The Snark Bible

The Snark Bible

A Reference Guide to Verbal Sparring, Comebacks, Irony, Insults, Sarcasm, and So Much More

Lawrence Dorfman

Skyhorse Publishing

All Rights Reserved. No part of this book may be reproduced in any manner without the express written consent of the publisher, except in the case of brief excerpts in critical reviews or articles. All inquiries should be addressed to Skyhorse Publishing, 307 West 36th Street, 11th Floor, New York, NY 10018.

Skyhorse Publishing books may be purchased in bulk at special discounts for sales promotion, corporate gifts, fund-raising, or educational purposes. Special editions can also be created to specifications. For details, contact the Special Sales Department, Skyhorse Publishing, 307 West 36th Street, 11th Floor, New York, NY 10018 or info@skyhorsepublishing.com.

Skyhorse® and Skyhorse Publishing® are registered trademarks of Skyhorse Publishing, Inc.®, a Delaware corporation.

Visit our website at www.skyhorsepublishing.com.

10 9 8 7 6 5 4 3 2 1

Library of Congress Cataloging-in-Publication Data is available on file.

Cover design by Owen Corrigan
Cover photo credit Thinkstock

ISBN: 978-1-62914-429-0
Ebook ISBN: 978-1-63220-129-4

Printed in China

CONTENTS

THE BOOK OF POLITICS

Musing Philosophic

Disbelief in magic can force a poor soul into believing in government
and business.
—TOM ROBBINS

✦✦✦

Never underestimate the ego of a politician.
—DAN BROWN

✦✦

The men the American people admire most extravagantly are the
most daring liars: the men they detest most violently are those that
try to tell the truth.
—H. L. MENCKEN

✦✦✦

The American political system is like fast food—mushy, insipid, made
out of disgusting parts of things . . . and everybody wants some.
—P. J. O'ROURKE

✦✦

Politics is a blood sport.
—ANEURIN BEVAN

+++

In politics, nothing happens by accident. If it happens, you can bet it was planned that way.
—FRANKLIN DELANO ROOSEVELT

++

Power draws the corrupted; absolute power would draw the absolutely corrupted.
—COLIN BARTH

+++

One of the little celebrated powers of presidents is to listen to their critics with just enough sympathy to ensure their silence.
—JOHN KENNETH GALBRAITH

++

When I was a boy I was told that anybody could become president; I'm beginning to believe it.
—CLARENCE DARROW

+++

Man cannot live by bread alone; he must have peanut butter.
—JAMES A. GARFIELD

++

POLITICS IS . . .

. . . the art of looking for trouble, finding it whether it exists or not, diagnosing it incorrectly, and applying the wrong remedy.
—GROUCHO MARX

+++

. . . the skilled use of blunt objects.
—LESTER B. PEARSON

++

. . . made up largely of irrelevancies.
—DALTON CAMP

+++

. . . perhaps the only profession for which no preparation is thought necessary.
—ROBERT LOUIS STEVENSON

++

. . . the art of preventing people from sticking their noses in things that are properly their business.
—PAUL VALERY

+++

. . . the art of postponing decisions until they are no longer relevant.
—HENRI QUEUILLE

++

. . . supposed to be the second oldest profession. I have come to realize that it bears a very close resemblance to the first.
—RONALD REAGAN

+++

. . . like football; if you see daylight, go through the hole.
—JOHN F. KENNEDY

Politics is not a bad profession. If you succeed there are many rewards, if you disgrace yourself . . . you can always write a book.
—RONALD REAGAN

✦✦

Politics is not the art of the impossible. It consists in choosing between the disastrous and the unpalatable.
—JOHN KENNETH GALBRAITH

✦✦✦

The right to be heard does not automatically include the right to be taken seriously.
—HUBERT HUMPHREY

✦✦

I always figured the American public wanted a solemn ass for president, so I went along with them.
—CALVIN COOLIDGE

✦✦✦

The vice presidency is like the last cookie on the plate. Everybody insists he won't take it, but somebody always does.
—BILL VAUGHAN

✦✦

The man with the best job in the country is the vice president. All he has to do is get up every morning and say, "How's the president?"
—WILL ROGERS

✦✦✦

On Democracy

Democracy means government by discussion, but it is only effective if you can stop people talking.
—CLEMENT ATLEE

◆◆

Democracy is a process by which the people are free to choose the man who will get all the blame.
—LAURENCE J. PETER

◆◆◆

The best argument against democracy is a five-minute conversation with the average voter.
—WINSTON CHURCHILL

◆◆

I believe democracy is our greatest export. At least until China figures out a way to stamp it out of plastic for three cents a unit.
—STEPHEN COLBERT

◆◆◆

Democracy means simply the bludgeoning of the people by the people for the people.
—OSCAR WILDE

◆◆

Democracy substitutes election by the incompetent many for appointment by the corrupt few.
—GEORGE BERNARD SHAW

When a man assumes a public trust, he should consider himself as public property.
—THOMAS JEFFERSON

✦✦✦

Always be sincere, even if you don't mean it.
—HARRY S. TRUMAN

✦✦

A fool and his money are soon elected.
—WILL ROGERS

✦✦✦

Everybody knows politics is a contact sport.
—BARACK OBAMA

✦✦

Forgive your enemies, but never forget their names.
—JOHN F. KENNEDY

✦✦✦

Mothers all want their sons to grow up to be president, but they don't want them to become politicians in the process.
—JOHN F. KENNEDY

✦✦

Being president is like running a cemetery: you've got a lot of people under you and nobody's listening.
—BILL CLINTON

✦✦✦

I have no ambition to govern men; it is a painful and thankless office.
—THOMAS JEFFERSON

◆◆

All the president is . . . is a glorified public relations man who spends
his time flattering, kissing, and kicking people to get them to do what
they are supposed to do anyway.
—HARRY S. TRUMAN

◆◆◆

The pay is good and I can walk to work.
—JOHN F. KENNEDY

◆◆

Oh, that lovely title, ex-president.
—DWIGHT D. EISENHOWER

◆◆◆

Capitalism is the astounding belief that the most wickedest of men
will do the most wickedest of things for the greatest good of everyone.
—JOHN MAYNARD KEYNES

◆◆

Apparently, a democracy is a place where numerous elections are held
at great cost without issues and with interchangeable candidates.
—GORE VIDAL

◆◆◆

The office of president is such a bastardized thing, half royalty and
half democracy that nobody knows whether to genuflect or spit.
—JIMMY BRESLIN

◆◆

Trying to get the presidency to work these days is like trying to sew buttons on a custard pie.
—JAMES BARBER

+++

Those that are too smart to engage in politics are punished by being governed by those who are dumber.
—PLATO

++

I have come to the conclusion that politics is too serious a matter to be left to the politicians.
—CHARLES DE GAULLE

+++

A man's got to believe in something. I believe I'll have another drink.
—W. C. FIELDS

++

A politician should have three hats. One for throwing into the ring, one for talking through, and one for pulling rabbits out of if elected.
—CARL SANDBURG

+++

Any American who is prepared to run for president should automatically, by definition, be disqualified from ever doing so.
—GORE VIDAL

++

One of the penalties for refusing to participate in politics is that you end up being governed by your inferiors.
—PLATO

+++

There is one thing about being president—no one can tell you when to sit down.
—DWIGHT D. EISENHOWER

++

Democracy is the art and science of running the circus from the monkey cage.
—H. L. MENCKEN

+++

There's nothing left . . . but to get drunk.
—FRANKLIN PIERCE,
AFTER LOSING THE DEMOCRATIC NOMINATION

++

Political language . . . is designed to make lies sound truthful and murder respectable, and to give an appearance of solidity to pure wind.
—GEORGE ORWELL

+++

In the lexicon of the political class, the word "sacrifice" means that the citizens are supposed to mail even more of their income to Washington so that the political class will not have to sacrifice the pleasure of spending it.
—GEORGE WILL

✦✦

Society is like a stew. If you don't stir it up every once in a while then a layer of scum floats to the top.
—EDWARD ABBEY

✦✦✦

Politics makes estranged bedfellows.
—GOODMAN ACE

✦✦

If a tree falls in a forest and lands on a politician, even if you can't hear the tree or the screams, I'll bet you'd at least hear the applause.
—PAUL TINDALE

✦✦✦

It has been said that democracy is the worst form of government except all the others that have been tried.
—WINSTON CHURCHILL

✦✦

You want a friend in Washington? Get a dog.
—HARRY S. TRUMAN

✦✦✦

Patriotism is a pernicious, psychopathic form of idiocy.
—GEORGE BERNARD SHAW

++

If you can't convince them, confuse them.
—HARRY TRUMAN

+++

When you reach the end of your rope, tie a knot in it and hang on.
—THOMAS JEFFERSON

++

Now I know what a statesman is; he's a dead politician. We need more statesmen.
—BOB EDWARDS

+++

The politicians were talking themselves red, white, and blue in the face.
—CLARE BOOTHE LUCE

++

Battle, n. A method of untying with the teeth a political knot that would not yield to the tongue.
—AMBROSE BIERCE

+++

Frankly, I don't mind not being president. I just mind that someone else is.
—EDWARD KENNEDY

++

Turn on to politics, or politics will turn on you.
—RALPH NADER

+++

Politicians are wonderful people as long as they stay away from things they don't understand, such as working for a living.
—P. J. O'ROURKE

++

Who Knows Who Said It?[1]

How come we choose from just two people to run for president and fifty for Miss America?

To succeed in politics, it is often necessary to rise above your principles.

Any sufficiently advanced bureaucracy is indistinguishable from molasses.

You know, sometimes, when they say you're ahead of your time, it's just a polite way of saying you have a real bad sense of timing.
—GEORGE MCGOVERN

+++

---

[1]   That's right, no one knows.

The whole aim of practical politics is to keep the populace alarmed (and hence clamorous to be led to safety) by menacing it with an endless series of hobgoblins, all of them imaginary.
—H. L. MENCKEN

++

There ain't no answer. There ain't gonna be any answer. There never has been an answer. That's the answer.
—GERTRUDE STEIN

+++

In diplomacy, an ultimatum is the last demand before concessions.
—AMBROSE BIERCE

++

Diplomacy—lying in state.
—OLIVER HERFORD

+++

Diplomacy is letting someone else have your way.
—LESTER PEARSON

++

A diplomat is a person who can tell you to go to hell in such a way that you actually look forward to the trip.
—CASKIE STINNETT

+++

Diplomacy is the art of saying "Nice doggie" until you can find a rock.
—WILL ROGERS

++

Democracy never lasts long. It soon wastes, exhausts, and murders itself. There never was a democracy yet that did not commit suicide.
—JOHN ADAMS

+++

Ninety percent of politicians give the other ten percent
a bad name.
—HENRY KISSINGER

++

Politicians are people who, when they see the light at the end of the tunnel, order more tunnel.
—SIR JOHN QUINTON

+++

Feeling good about government is like looking on the bright side of any catastrophe. When you quit looking on the bright side, the catastrophe is still there.
—P. J. O'ROURKE

++

The government is like a baby's alimentary canal, with a happy appetite at one end and no responsibility at the other.
—RONALD REAGAN

+++

We live in a world in which politics has replaced philosophy.
—MARTIN L. GROSS

++

There are many men of principle in both parties in America, but there is no party of principle.
—ALEXIS DE TOCQUEVILLE

+++

A politician . . . one that would circumvent God.
—WILLIAM SHAKESPEARE

++

A politician needs the ability to foretell what is going to happen tomorrow, next week, next month, and next year. And to have the ability afterwards to explain why it didn't happen.
—WINSTON CHURCHILL

+++

There are two things that are important in politics. The first is money . . . and I can't remember what the other one is.
—F. PAUL WILSON

++

All the people who really know how to run the country are busy driving taxicabs and cutting hair.
—GEORGE BURNS

+++

I think that all good, right thinking people in this country are sick and tired of being told that all good, right thinking people in this country are fed up with being told that all good, right thinking people in this country are fed up with being sick and tired. I'm certainly not, and I'm sick and tired of being told that I am.

—MONTY PYTHON

++

Anyone who believes exponential growth can go on forever in a finite world is either a madman or an economist.

—KENNETH BOULDING

+++

What this country needs are more unemployed politicians.

—EDWARD LANGLEY

++

American politicians will do anything for money; English politicians will take the money and won't do anything.

—STEPHEN LEACOCK

+++

The imbecility of men is always inviting the impudence of power.

—RALPH WALDO EMERSON

++

I can give you 1,040 good reasons why I hate the government.

—TERRI GUILLEMETS

~+~

Q. Are we EVER going to have a federal tax system that regular people can understand?

A. Our top political leaders have all voiced strong support for this idea.

Q. So you're saying it will never happen?

A. Pretty much.

~+~

The problem of power is how to get men of power to live for the public rather than off the public.
—ROBERT F. KENNEDY

+++

All political lives, unless they are cut off in midstream at a happy juncture, end in failure, because that is the nature of politics and of human affairs.
—ENOCH POWELL

++

The enemy isn't conservatism.
The enemy isn't liberalism. The enemy is bullshit.
—LARS-ERIK NELSON

+++

I Am Not a Crook

I haven't committed a crime. What I did was fail to comply with the
law.
—DAVID DINKINS

✦✦✦

We hang the petty thieves and appoint the great ones to public office.
—AESOP

✦✦

I was really too honest a man to be a politician and live.
—SOCRATES

✦✦✦

Believe nothing until it has been officially denied.
—CLAUDE COCKBURN

✦✦

Rutherford B. Hayes: His Fraudulency.
—ANONYMOUS

✦✦✦

He is such an infernal liar.
—U. S. GRANT [ON ANDREW JOHNSON]

✦✦

Filthy storyteller, despot, liar, thief, braggart, buffoon, usurper,
monster, ignoramus Abe, old scoundrel, perjurer, swindler, tyrant,
field-butcher, land-pirate . . .
—HARPER'S MAGAZINE [ON ABRAHAM LINCOLN]

✦✦✦

Turnacoat Tyler.
—POPULAR SLOGAN OF THE DAY [ABOUT JOHN TYLER]

✦✦

I would have made a good Pope!
—RICHARD M. NIXON

✦✦✦

There are a lot of people who lie and get away with it,
and that's just a fact.
—DONALD RUMSFELD

✦✦

He is ignorant, passionate, hypocritical, corrupt, and easily swayed by
the basest men who surround him.
—HENRY CLAY [ON ANDREW JACKSON]

✦✦✦

In Louisiana we don't bet on football games, we bet on whether a
politician is going to be indicted or not.
—MARK DUFFY

++

I would not like to be a political leader in Russia. They never know
when they're being taped.
—RICHARD NIXON

+++

If one morning I walked on top of the water across the Potomac River,
the headline that afternoon would read: 'President Can't Swim."'
LYNDON JOHNSON

++

If I were two-faced, would I be wearing this one?
—ABRAHAM LINCOLN

+++

Over the years the quality of our presidential timber has declined;
today we are pretty much satisfied if our president stays out of jail and
occasionally emits a complete sentence.
—DAVE BARRY

++

Crime does not pay . . . as well as politics.
—ALFRED E. NEWMAN

+++

One way to make sure crime doesn't pay would be
to let the government run it.
—RONALD REAGAN

++

Politicians are wedded to the truth, but unlike many other married
couples they sometimes live apart.
—SAKI

+++

A good politician is quite as unthinkable as an honest burglar.
—H. L. MENCKEN

++

I have certain rules I live by. My first rule: I don't believe anything the
government tells me.
—GEORGE CARLIN

+++

It's useless to hold anyone to anything he says while he's in love,
drunk, or running for office.
—SHIRLEY MACLAINE

~+~

Q: How long does a Congressman serve?
A: Depends on his sentence.

~+~

Instead of giving a politician the keys to the city, it might be better to change the locks.
—DOUG LARSON

++

The cardinal rule of politics—never get caught in bed with a live man or a dead woman.
—J. R. EWING

+++

When a politician changes his position it's sometimes hard to tell whether he has seen the light or felt the heat.
—ROBERT FUOSS

++

The infectiousness of crime is like that of the plague.
—NAPOLEON BONAPARTE

+++

In a closed society where everybody's guilty, the only crime is getting caught. In a world of thieves, the only final sin is stupidity.
—HUNTER S. THOMPSON

++

The only power any government has is the power to crack down on criminals. Well, when there aren't enough criminals, one makes them. One declares so many things to be a crime that it becomes impossible for men to live without breaking laws.
—AYN RAND

+++

What $50,000 Will Buy You In Washington, DC[2]

- ↔ 2 First Class tickets to Cabo, luggage included
- ↔ 2 seats in the Senate
- ↔ 4 seats in the House
- ↔ 6 seats at a Bruce Springsteen concert (first 10 rows)
- ↔ 3,547 "World's Best Lobbyist" mugs
- ↔ A 2:00 p.m. Tee Time at St. Andrews
- ↔ Half of a diamond encrusted thong
- ↔ Skybox tickets at any arena in America
- ↔ A life-size replica of yourself in LEGO blocks
- ↔ Your own war
- ↔ Vegas, baby

Organized crime in America takes in over forty billion dollars a year and spends very little on office supplies.
—WOODY ALLEN

++

---

[2] With the right lobbyist

Homosexuality in Russia is a crime and the punishment is seven years in prison, locked up with the other men. There is a three-year waiting list.
—YAKOV SMIRNOFF

+++

Nixon told us he was going to take crime out of the streets. He did. He took it into the damn White House.
—RALPH ABERNATHY

++

A politician can appear to have his nose to the grindstone while straddling a fence and keeping both ears to the ground.
—ANONYMOUS

+++

The reason there are so few female politicians is that it is too much trouble to put makeup on two faces.
—MAUREEN MURPHY

++

As a rule of thumb, if the government wants you to know it, it probably isn't true.
—CRAIG MURRAY

+++

Democracy is defended in three stages. Ballot Box, Jury Box, Cartridge Box.
—AMBROSE BIERCE

++

Bureaucracy defends the status quo long past the time when the quo has lost its status.
—LAURENCE J. PETER

+++

The illegal we do immediately. The unconstitutional takes a little longer.
—HENRY KISSINGER

++

The truth is a frequent casualty in the heat of an election campaign.
—TIP O'NEILL

+++

Avoid all needle drugs. The only dope worth shooting is Richard Nixon.
—ABBIE HOFFMAN

++

Nixon impeached himself. He gave us Gerald Ford as his revenge.
—BELLA ABZUG

+++

He is a man of his most recent word.
—WILLIAM F. BUCKLEY [ON LYNDON JOHNSON]

++

No man's life, liberty, or property is safe while the legislature is in session.
—MARK TWAIN

+++

When you start looking for some politician's footprints on the sands
of time, steer for the mud holes first.
—ROBERT ELLIOTT GONZALES

✦✦

Politics: the art of appearing candid and completely open while
concealing as much as possible.
—FRANK HERBERT, IN *DUNE*

✦✦✦

Political language . . . is designed to make lies sound truthful and
murder respectable.
—GEORGE ORWELL

✦✦

People always ask me, "Where were you when Kennedy got shot?" . . .
Well, I don't have an alibi.
—EMO PHILIPS

✦✦✦

If a politician murders his mother, the first response of the press or of
his opponents will likely be not that it was a terrible thing to do, but
rather that in a statement made six years before he had gone on record
as being opposed to matricide.
—MEG GREENFIELD

✦✦

There is no kind of dishonesty into which otherwise good people
more easily and frequently fall than that of defrauding the
government.
—BENJAMIN FRANKLIN

✦✦✦

Whenever a man has cast a longing eye on offices, a rottenness begins in his conduct.
—THOMAS JEFFERSON

✦✦

Son, if you can't take their money, drink their whiskey, screw their women, and then vote against 'em, you don't deserve to be here.
—SAM RAYBURN, FORMER SPEAKER OF THE HOUSE

✦✦✦

When the president does it, it means it's not illegal.
—RICHARD NIXON

✦✦

Washington, DC is to lying what Wisconsin is to cheese.
—DENNIS MILLER

✦✦✦

I don't care who does the electing just so long as I do the nominating.
—WILLIAM "BOSS" TWEED[3]

✦✦

It is hard to believe that a man is telling the truth when you know that you would lie if you were in his place.
—H. L. MENCKEN

✦✦✦

---

3   The most corrupt American politician of the nineteenth century

"Reform" is a word you always oughta' watch out for. "Reform" is a change that you're supposed to like. And watch it—as soon as you hear the word "reform," you [should] reach for your wallet and see who's lifting it.
—NOAM CHOMSKY

++

People demand freedom of speech as a compensation for the freedom of thought, which they never use.
—SØREN AABYE KIERKEGAARD

+++

If they can get you asking the wrong questions, they don't have to worry about the answers.
—THOMAS PYNCHON

++

I either want less corruption, or more chance to participate in it.
—ASHLEIGH BRILLIANT

+++

I'm spending a year dead for tax reasons.
—DOUGLAS ADAMS

++

When they call the roll in the Senate, the Senators do not know whether to answer "present" or "not guilty."
—TEDDY ROOSEVELT

+++

War and Other Ways to Make a Statement

War, n: A time-tested political tactic guaranteed to raise a president's popularity rating by at least thirty points. It is especially useful during election years and economic downturns.
—CHAZ BUFE

+++

The reason the American Army does so well in wartime is that war is chaos, and the American Army practices it on a daily basis.
—GERMAN GENERAL

++

Anything worth fighting for is worth fighting dirty for.
—ANONYMOUS

+++

I haven't heard the president state that we're at war. That's why I too do not know—do we use the term "intervention"? Do we use "war"? Do we use "squirmish"? What is it?
—SARAH PALIN, ON LIBYA

++

Rear, n. In American military matters, that exposed part of the army that is nearest to Congress.
—AMBROSE BIERCE

+++

War makes rattling good history; but peace is poor reading.
—THOMAS HARDY

++

We have women in the military, but they don't put us in the front lines. They don't know if we can fight, if we can kill. I think we can. All the general has to do is walk over to the women and say, "You see the enemy over there? They say you look fat in those uniforms."
—ELAYNE BOOSLER

+++

It will be a great day when our schools have all the money they need, and our air force has to have a bake sale to buy a bomber.
—ROBERT FULGHUM

++

We, the willing, led by the unknowing, are doing the impossible for the ungrateful. We have now done so much for so long with so little, we are now capable of doing anything with nothing.
—ANONYMOUS

+++

We are not retreating—we are advancing in another direction.
—GENERAL DOUGLAS MACARTHUR

++

Match the President to His War[4]

A. George Washington   F. Woodrow Wilson
B. James Madison   G. Franklin D. Roosevelt
C. James Monroe   H. Harry Truman
D. James Polk   I. George H. Bush
E. William McKinley   J. George W. Bush

~ ◆ ~

1. The Revolutionary War (1775–1783)
2. Iraqi Invasion and Occupation (2003 . . .)
3. World War II (1939–1945)
4. War of 1812
5. Korean War (1950–1953)
6. Persian Gulf War I with Iraq (1990)
7. World War I (1914–1918)
8. Spanish-American War (1898)
9. Mexican War (1846–1848)
10. Indian Wars of 1817

You really can't blame the military for wanting to go to war [in Iraq].
They've got all these new toys and they want to know whether they
work or not.

—ANDY ROONEY

◆ ◆ ◆

---

[4]   1. A, 2. J, 3. G, 4. B, 5. H, 6. I, 7. F, 8. E, 9. D, 10. C

Before a war, military science seems a real science, like astronomy; but after a war, it seems more like astrology.
—REBECCA WEST

++

The Army has carried the American . . . ideal to its logical conclusion. Not only do they prohibit discrimination on the grounds of race, creed, and color, but also on ability.
—TOM LEHRER

+++

We have twelve thousand troops. But that's not enough. That's the amount that is going to die. And at the end of a war you need some soldiers left, really, or else it looks like you've lost.
—GENERAL GEORGE MILLER FROM "IN THE LOOP"

++

Make the lie big, make it simple, keep saying it, and eventually they will believe it.
—ADOLPH HITLER

+++

I only know two tunes: One of them is "Yankee Doodle" and the other isn't.
—ULYSSES S. GRANT

++

O peace! How many wars were waged in thy name?
—ALEXANDER POPE

+++

A great war leaves a country with three armies: an army of cripples,
an army of mourners, and an army of thieves.
—ANONYMOUS

++

The world cannot continue to wage war like physical giants and to
seek peace like intellectual pygmies.
—BASIL O'CONNOR

+++

If this were a dictatorship, it'd be a heck of a lot easier, just so long as
I'm the dictator.
—GEORGE W. BUSH

++

"My country right or wrong" is like saying, "My mother drunk or
sober."
—G. K. CHESTERTON

+++

Military justice is to justice what military music is to music.
—GROUCHO MARX

++

A visitor from Mars could easily pick out the civilized nations. They
have the best implements of war.
—HERBERT PROCHNOW

+++

The object of war is not to die for your country but to make the other bastard die for his.
—GENERAL GEORGE PATTON

✦✦

My hope is that gays will be running the world, because then there would be no war. Just a greater emphasis on military apparel.
—ROSEANNE BARR

✦✦✦

A prisoner of war is a man who tries to kill you and fails, and then asks you not to kill him.
—WINSTON CHURCHILL

✦✦

Nothing is so admirable in politics as a short memory.
—JOHN KENNETH GALBRAITH

✦✦✦

Pentagon records show that at least eight thousand members of the all-volunteer US Army have deserted since the Iraq war began. Hey, at least somebody has an exit strategy.
—TINA FEY

✦✦

Asking an incumbent member of Congress to vote for term limits is a bit like asking a chicken to vote for Colonel Sanders.
—BOB INGLIS

✦✦✦

Sen. Hillary Clinton called for President Bush to begin pulling troops out of Iraq next year. And let me tell you something, when it comes to telling a president when to pull out, no one has more experience than Hillary Clinton.

—JAY LENO

◆◆

Military intelligence is a contradiction in terms.

—GROUCHO MARX

~◆~

George Bush started an ill-timed and disastrous war under false pretenses by lying to the American people and to the Congress; he ran a budget surplus into a severe deficit; he consistently and unconscionably favored the wealthy and corporations over the rights and needs of the population; he destroyed trust and confidence in, and good will toward, the United States around the globe; he ignored global warming, to the world's detriment; he wantonly broke our treaty obligations; he condoned torture of prisoners; he attempted to create a theocracy in the United States and appointed incompetent cronies to positions of vital national importance.

So, why didn't someone just give him a blow job so we could impeach him?

~◆~

The only way to reduce the number of nuclear weapons is to use them.
—RUSH LIMBAUGH

+++

Why does the Air Force need expensive new bombers? Have the people we've been bombing over the years been complaining?
—GEORGE WALLACE

++

We do know of certain knowledge that he [Osama Bin Laden] is either in Afghanistan, or in some other country, or dead.
—DONALD RUMSFELD (IN 2003)

+++

Government is the Entertainment division of the military-industrial complex.
—FRANK ZAPPA

++

The Homeland Security System. They had it color-coded, like we're in elementary school. Simplify it, there should be just three levels of security: Jesus Christ, Goddammit, and FUCK ME!
—LEWIS BLACK

+++

All war is deception.
—SUN TZU

++

"War . . . What is it good for? Absolutely nothing."
—EDWIN STARR

+++

We found the term "killing" too broad.
—STATE DEPARTMENT SPOKESPERSON ON WHY THE WORD
"KILLING" WAS REPLACED WITH "UNLAWFUL OR ARBITRARY
DEPRIVATION OF LIFE"

++

From a marketing point of view, you don't roll out new products in
August.
—WHITE HOUSE CHIEF OF STAFF ANDREW CARD ON WHY THE
BUSH ADMINISTRATION WAITED UNTIL AFTER LABOR DAY TO
TRY TO SELL THE AMERICAN PEOPLE ON WAR AGAINST IRAQ

+++

War is God's way of teaching Americans geography.
—AMBROSE BIERCE

++

Sixty years ago Hitler invaded Poland. This led to the creation of The
History Channel.
—JAY LENO

+++

I detest war; it ruins conversation.
—BERNARD FONTENELLE

++

The Gulf War was like teenage sex. We got in too
soon and out too soon.
—TOM HARKIN

✦✦✦

In times of disorder and stress, the fanatics play a prominent role; in
times of peace, the critics. Both are shot after the revolution.
—EDMUND WILSON

✦✦

A patriot must always be ready to defend his country against his
government.
—EDWARD ABBEY

✦✦✦

THE BOOK OF
WORK & PLAY

Work

One of the symptoms of an approaching nervous breakdown is the belief that one's work is terribly important.
—BERTRAND RUSSELL

+++

The brain is a wonderful organ. It starts working the moment you get up in the morning and does not stop until you get into the office.
—ROBERT FROST

++

Hard work is damn near as overrated as monogamy.
—HUEY LONG

+++

Disobedience, n. The silver lining to the cloud of servitude.
—AMBROSE BIERCE

++

What do hookers do on their nights off—type?
—ELAYNE BOOSLER

+++

I always arrive late at the office, but I make up for it by leaving early.
—CHARLES LAMB

Workplace Commentary

> ➢ This isn't an office; it's hell with fluorescent lighting.

> ➢ The fact that no one understands you doesn't mean you're an artist.

> ➢ I have plenty of talent and vision. I just don't care.

> ➢ I like you. You remind me of when I was young and stupid.

> ➢ I'm not being rude. You're just insignificant.

> ➢ I'm already visualizing the duct tape over your mouth.

> ➢ I will always cherish the initial misconceptions I had about you.

> ➢ It's a thankless job, but I've got a lot of karma to burn off.

> ➢ How about never? Is never good for you?

> ➢ I'm really easy to get along with once you people learn to worship me.

> ➢ I'll try being nicer if you'll try being smarter.

> ➢ I might look like I'm doing nothing, but at the cellular level, I'm really quite busy.

> ➢ I see you've set aside this special time to humiliate yourself in public.

- ➢ Someday, we'll look back on this, laugh nervously, and change the subject.

- ➢ If you find it hard to laugh at yourself, I would be happy to do it for you.

- ➢ Sorry, I can't hear you over the sound of how awesome I am.

- ➢ I don't work here. I'm a consultant.

- ➢ How do I set the laser printer to stun?

- ➢ Who, me? I just wander from room to room.

~✦~

A young man hired by a supermarket reported for his first day of work. The manager greeted him with a warm handshake and a smile, gave him a broom, and said, "Your first job will be to sweep out the store."

"But I'm a college graduate," the young man replied indignantly.

"Oh, I'm sorry. I didn't know that," said the manager. "Here, give me the broom—I'll show you how."

~✦~

Beware the lollipop of mediocrity; lick it once and you'll suck forever.

—BRIAN WILSON

✦✦

There is no *I* in *team*, but there are four in *platitude-quoting idiot.*
—ANONYMOUS

✦✦✦

Some people see things that are and ask, *Why?*
Some people dream of things that never were
and ask, *Why not?* Some people have to go to work and don't have
time for all that shit.
—GEORGE CARLIN

~✦~

*A guy walked into the local welfare office to pick up his
check. He marched straight up to the counter and said,
"Hi. You know, I just HATE drawing welfare. I'd really
rather have a job."*

*The social worker behind the counter said, "Your
timing is excellent. We just got a job opening from a very
wealthy old man who wants a chauffeur and bodyguard
for his beautiful daughter. You'll have to drive around
in his Mercedes, and he'll supply all of your clothes. Because of the long hours, meals will be provided. You'll be
expected to escort the daughter on her overseas holiday
trips, and you will have to satisfy her sexual urges. You'll
be provided a two-bedroom apartment above the garage.
The salary is $200,000 a year."*

The guy, wide-eyed, said, "You're bullshittin' me!"

*The social worker said, "Yeah, well . . . you started
it."*

~✦~

The Boss

- I didn't say it was your fault. I said I was going to blame it on you.

- We passed over a lot of good people to get the ones we hired.

- My boss said to me, "What you see as a glass ceiling, I see as a protective barrier."

- He's given automobile accident victims new hope for recovery.

- He walks, talks, and performs rudimentary tasks, all without the benefit of a spine.

- To err is human, to blame somebody else shows good management skills.

- Some people climb the ladder of success. My boss walked under it.

- My idea of a team effort is a lot of people doing whatever I say.

- HR manager to job candidate: "I see you've had no computer training. Although that qualifies you for upper management, it means you're underqualified for our entry-level positions."

Snarky Behavior at Work[5]

> When someone asks you to do something, ask if they want that supersized.

> Phone someone in the office you barely know, leave your name, and say, "Just called to say I can't talk right now. Bye."

> To signal the end of a conversation, clamp your hands over your ears and grimace.

> When someone hands you a piece of paper, finger it and whisper huskily, "Mmmmmmm, that feels soooooo good!"

> Say to your boss, "I like your style," and shoot him with double-barreled fingers.

> Kneel in front of the watercooler and drink directly from the nozzle.

> Shout random numbers while someone is counting.

> At the end of a meeting, suggest that, for once, it would be nice to conclude with the singing of the national anthem (extra points if you actually launch into it yourself).

> After every sentence, say *mon* in a really bad Jamaican accent. As in, "The report's on your desk, mon." Keep this up for one hour.

> While a coworker is out, move his or her chair into the elevator.

> In a meeting or crowded situation, slap your forehead repeatedly and mutter, "Shut up! *Please!* All of you just shut up!"

---

[5]   There is some physical snark involved here. Consult your doctor. Or not.

- Carry your keyboard over to your colleague and ask if he wants to trade.
- Repeat the following conversation ten times to the same person: "Do you hear that?" "What?" "Never mind, it's gone now."
- Come to work in army fatigues and when asked why, say, "I can't talk about it."
- Posing as a maitre d', call a colleague and tell him he's won a lunch for four at a local restaurant. Let him go.
- During the course of a meeting, slowly edge your chair toward the door.
- Arrange toy figures on the table to represent each meeting attendee, and move them according to the movements of their real-life counterparts.
- Page yourself over the intercom (don't disguise your voice).
- Encourage your colleagues to join you in a little synchronized chair dancing.
- Put your garbage can on your desk and label it IN.
- Reply to everything someone says with, "That's what you think."
- Finish all your sentences with "in accordance with the prophecy."
- Send email to the rest of the company to tell them what you're doing. For example: "If anyone needs me, I'll be in the bathroom."
- Put mosquito netting around your cubicle.

Business conventions are important because they demonstrate how many people a company can operate without.
—ANONYMOUS

✦✦

I used to be a lifeguard, but some blue kid got me fired.
—ANONYMOUS

✦✦✦

I wish my brother would learn a trade, so I would know what kind of work he's out of.
—HENNY YOUNGMAN

✦✦

A motivational sign at work: THE BEATINGS WILL CONTINUE UNTIL MORALE IMPROVES.
—ANONYMOUS

✦✦✦

Studies show that more information is passed through watercooler gossip than through official memos, which puts me at a disadvantage because I bring my own water to work.
—DWIGHT SCHRUTE, *THE OFFICE*

~✦~

A bum asked, "Give me $20 'til payday?" I asked, "When's payday?" He said, "I don't know. You're the one who's working!"

~✦~

"Looks like you've been missing a lot of work lately." "I wouldn't say
I've been *missing* it, Bob."
—*OFFICE SPACE*

✦✦

I'll be happy to make these unnecessary changes to this irrelevant
document.
—*DILBERT*

✦✦✦

Tell me what you need, and I'll tell you how to get along without it.
—*DILBERT*

✦✦

Normal is getting dressed in clothes that you buy for work and
driving through traffic in a car that you are still paying for—in order
to get to the job you need to pay for the clothes and the car, and the
house you leave vacant all day so you can afford to live in it.
—ELLEN DEGENERES

✦✦✦

Because right now, this is a job. If I advance any higher, this would
be my career. And if this were my career, I'd have to throw myself in
front of a train.
—JIM HALPERT, *THE OFFICE*

✦✦

~+~

A guy goes to the post office to apply for a job. The interviewer asks him, "Have you been in the service?"

"Yes," he says. "I was in the armed forces for three years."

The interviewer says, "That will give you extra points toward employment." He then asks, "Are you disabled in any way?"

The guy says, "Yes, 100 percent. A mortar round exploded near me and blew my testicles off."

The interviewer tells the guy, "OK, I can hire you right now. The hours are from 8:00 a.m. till 5:00 p.m. You can start tomorrow. Come in at 10:00 a.m."

The guy is puzzled and says, "If the hours are from 8:00 a.m. to 5:00 p.m., then why do you want me to come in at 10:00 a.m.?"

"This is a government job," the interviewer says. "For the first two hours, we stand around scratching our balls. No point in you coming in for that."

~+~

Ham and eggs is just a day's work for the chicken
but a lifetime commitment for the pig.
—ANONYMOUS

♦♦♦

The easiest job in the world has to be coroner. Surgery on dead
people. What's the worst thing that could happen? If everything went
wrong, maybe you'd get a pulse.
—DENNIS MILLER

♦♦

The trouble with unemployment is that the minute you wake up in
the morning, you're on the job.
—SLAPPY WHITE

♦♦♦

Your Performance Review

> ➤ Never give me work in the morning. Always wait until 4 p.m. and then bring it in to me. The challenge of a deadline is refreshing.

> ➤ If it's a rush job, run in and interrupt me every ten minutes to inquire how I am doing. That helps. Or even better, hover behind me, advising me at every keystroke.

> ➤ Always leave without telling anyone where you are going. It gives me a chance to be creative when someone asks where you are.

> ➤ If my arms are full of papers, boxes, books, or supplies, don't open the door for me. I need to learn how to function as a paraplegic, and opening doors with no arms is good training.

> ➤ If you give me more than one job to do, don't tell me which is the priority. I am psychic.

> ➤ Do your best to keep me late. I adore this office and really have nowhere to go or anything to do. I have no life beyond work.

> ➤ If a job I do pleases you, keep it a secret. If that gets out, it could mean a promotion.

> ➤ If you don't like my work, tell everyone. I like my name to be popular in conversations. I was born to be whipped.

> If you have special instructions for a job, don't write them down. In fact, save them until the job is almost done. No use confusing me with useful information.

> Never introduce me to people you are with. I have no right to know anything. In the corporate food chain, I am plankton. When you refer to them later, my shrewd deductions will identify them.

> Be nice to me only when the job I am doing for you could really change your life and send you straight to manager's hell.

> Tell me all your little problems. No one else has any, and it's nice to know someone is less fortunate. I especially like the story about having to pay so much tax on the bonus check you received for being such a good manager.

> Wait until my yearly review and *then* tell me what my goal *should* have been.

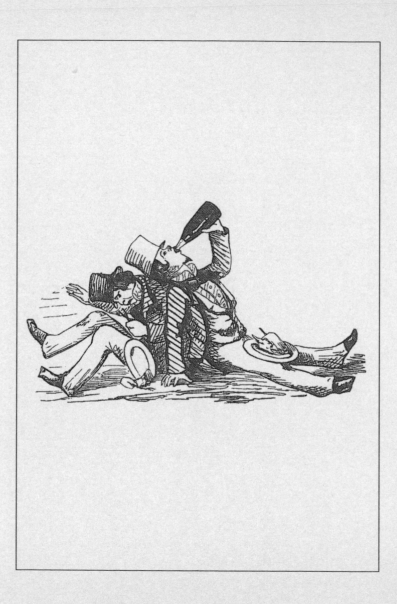

Drugs, Drinking, and the Law

Bacchus, n. A convenient deity invented by the
ancients as an excuse for getting drunk.
—AMBROSE BIERCE

♦♦

The problem with some people is that when
they're not drunk, they're sober.
—WILLIAM BUTLER YEATS

♦♦♦

I envy people who drink. At least they have
something to blame everything on.
—OSCAR LEVANT

♦♦

You're not drunk if you can lie on the floor
without holding on.
—DEAN MARTIN

♦♦♦

When I read about the evils of drinking, I gave up reading.
—HENNY YOUNGMAN

~•~

A drunk walks into a bar, clearly shit-faced. The bartender refuses to serve him. Five minutes later, he comes in again through a side door, but again, the bartender refuses him service. A few minutes later, the drunk comes in the back door, and again, the barkeep refuses to serve him.

"Jesus, man. How many bars do you work at?"

~•~

The trouble with jogging is that the
ice falls out of your glass.
—MARTIN MULL

••

Back in my drinking days, I would tremble and shake for hours upon arising. It was the only exercise I got.
—W. C. FIELDS

•••

Oh, I'm in no condition to drive. Wait a minute. I don't have to listen to myself. I'm drunk.
—HOMER SIMPSON, *THE SIMPSONS*

Written over a Urinal in a Bar

> ➤ Express Lane: Five beers or less.

> ➤ What are you looking up on the wall for?
> The joke is in your hands.

Warning: Liquor Can . . .

> ➤ Make you believe that ex-lovers are really dying for you to telephone them at four o'clock in the morning.

> ➤ Be a major factor in dancing like an asshole.

> ➤ Cause you to tell the same boring story over and over again until your friends want to smash your head in.

> ➤ Leave you wondering what the hell ever happened to your underwear.

> ➤ Create the illusion that you are tougher, more handsome, and smarter than some really, really, really big biker guy named Bubba.

> ➤ Make you think you are whispering when you are not.

> ➤ Make you think you can seduce members of the opposite sex.

> ➤ Lead you to think people are laughing *with* you.

> ➤ Actually *cause* pregnancy.

I know I'm drinking myself to a slow death,
but then I'm in no hurry.
—ROBERT BENCHLEY

✦✦

In a study, scientists report that drinking beer can be
good for the liver. I'm sorry, did I say "scientists"?
I meant "Irish people."
—TINA FEY

✦✦✦

~✦~

Q: Where does an Irish family go on vacation?
A: A different bar.

~✦~

I'm on a whiskey diet. I've lost three days already.
—TOMMY COOPER

✦✦

I always wake up at the crack of ice.
—JOE E. LEWIS

~✦~

A drunk phoned the police to report that thieves had
been in his car. "They've stolen the dashboard, the steer-
ing wheel, the brake pedal, even the accelerator!" he cried
out. "Hey, wise guy," the cop replied. "Why don't you try
getting in the front seat?"

~✦~

An intelligent man is sometimes forced to be
drunk to spend time with fools.
—ERNEST HEMINGWAY

+++

A woman drove me to drink and I didn't even have the
decency to thank her.

—W. C. FIELDS

++

If you drink, don't drive. Don't even putt.
—DEAN MARTIN

+++

Reality Check

- A bartender is a pharmacist with a limited inventory.

- Drugs may lead to nowhere, but at least it's the scenic route.

- I'm not addicted to cocaine. I just like the way it smells.

- I tried snorting Coke once, but the ice cubes got stuck in my nose.

- Time is never wasted when you're wasted all the time.

- Rehab is for quitters.

I don't like people who take drugs.
Customs men for example.
—MICK MILLER

♦♦

I don't use drugs—my dreams are frightening enough.
—M. C. ESCHER

♦♦♦

Don't do drugs because if you do drugs you'll go to prison, and drugs
are really expensive in prison.
—JOHN HARDWICK

♦♦

I would never do crack. I would never do a drug named after a part of
my own ass, okay?
—DENIS LEARY

♦♦♦

Cocaine is God's way of saying you're
making too much money.
—ROBIN WILLIAMS

♦♦

This is your brain? I've seen a lot of weird
shit on drugs. I have never looked at a fucking
egg and thought it was a brain.
—BILL HICKS

♦♦♦

If A Cop Pulls You Over . . . [6]

> ➤ Are you Andy or Barney?

> ➤ Don't you know why you pulled me over? Okay, just so one of us does.

> ➤ I thought you had to be in good physical condition to be a police officer.

> ➤ You're not gonna check the trunk, are you?

> ➤ *Obstruction of justice?* No sir, I prefer to think of it as "avoiding complications."

> ➤ And when the officer says, "Your eyes look red. Have you been drinking?" you probably shouldn't respond with, "Your eyes look glazed. Have you been eating doughnuts?"

I've been doing the Fonda workout: the Peter Fonda workout. That's where I wake up, take a hit of acid, smoke a joint, and run to my sister's house and ask her for money.

—KEVIN MEANEY

++

---

[6] All of which will get you arrested, beaten, or both—knowing when to snark is a highly desirable quality and skill.

Cop Snark Backatcha

> ➢ Relax; the handcuffs are tight because they're new. They'll stretch out after you wear them awhile.

> ➢ Take your hands off the car, and I'll make your birth certificate a worthless document.

> ➢ If you run, you'll only go to jail tired.

> ➢ Can you run faster than 1,200 feet per second? In case you didn't know, that is the average speed of a 9mm bullet fired from my gun.

> ➢ So you don't know how fast you were going. I guess that means I can write anything I want on the ticket, huh?

> ➢ No, sir, we don't have quotas anymore. We used to have quotas but now we're allowed to write as many tickets as we want.

> ➢ I'm glad to hear the chief of police is a good personal friend of yours. At least you know someone who can post your bail.

> ➢ You didn't think we give pretty women tickets? You're right, we don't.

I hate to advocate drugs, alcohol, violence, or insanity to anyone, but
they've always worked for me.
—HUNTER S. THOMPSON

✦✦✦

People like you are the reason people like
me need medication.
—CHARLIE BARTLETT

✦✦

I've never had a problem with drugs.
I've had problems with the police.
KEITH RICHARDS

✦✦✦

If life is a waste of time, and time is a waste of life, then let's all get
wasted and have the time of our lives.
—ANONYMOUS

✦✦

~✦~

A police patrol car was parked outside a bar in Austin, Texas. After last call, the officer noticed a man leaving the bar apparently so intoxicated that he could barely walk. The man stumbled around the parking lot for a few minutes, with the officer quietly observing. After what seemed an eternity in which he tried his keys on five different vehicles, the man managed to find his car and fall into it.

He sat there for a few minutes as a number of other patrons left the bar and drove off.

Finally he started the car, switched the wipers on and off—it was a fine, dry summer night—flicked the blinkers on and off a couple of times, honked the horn, and then switched on the lights.

He moved the vehicle forward a few inches, reversed a little, and then remained still for a few more minutes as some more of the other patrons' vehicles left. At last, when his was the only car left in the parking lot, he pulled out and drove slowly down the road. The police officer, having waited patiently all this time, now started up his patrol car, put on the flashing lights, promptly pulled the man over, and administered a Breathalyzer test. To his amazement, the Breathalyzer indicated no evidence that the man had consumed any alcohol at all!

Dumbfounded, the officer said, "I'll have to ask you to accompany me to the police station. This Breathalyzer equipment must be broken."

"I doubt it," said the truly proud redneck. "Tonight I'm the designated decoy."

~+~

Movies

Oscar is eighty this year, which makes him now automatically the
front-runner for the Republican nomination.
—JON STEWART

+++

It's a scientific fact. For every year a person lives in
Hollywood, they lose two points of their IQ.
—TRUMAN CAPOTE

++

Acting is all about honesty. If you can
fake that, you've got it made.
—GEORGE BURNS

+++

Start every day off with a smile and get it over with.
—W. C. FIELDS

++

Behind the phony tinsel of Hollywood lies the real tinsel.
—OSCAR LEVANT

+++

You could put all the talent I had into your left eye and you would still not suffer from impaired vision.
—VERONICA LAKE

✦✦

Hollywood is a sewer with service from the Ritz.
—WILSON MIZNER

Lessons from the Movies

1. It is always possible to park directly outside any building you are visiting.

2. A detective can only solve a case once he has been suspended from duty.

3. Most laptop computers are powerful enough to override the communication systems of any invading alien civilization.

4. It does not matter if you are heavily outnumbered in a fight involving martial arts. Your enemies will wait patiently to attack you one by one by dancing around in a threatening manner until you have knocked out their predecessors.

5. When a person is knocked unconscious by a blow to the head, they will never suffer a concussion or brain damage.

6. No one involved in a car chase, hijacking, explosion, volcanic eruption, or alien invasion will ever go into shock.

7. Any lock can be picked by a credit card or a paper clip in seconds, unless it's the door to a burning building with a child trapped inside.

8. An electric fence powerful enough to kill a dinosaur will cause no lasting damage to an eight-year-old child.

9. Television news bulletins usually contain a story that affects you personally at that precise moment you turn the television on.

10. During all police investigations, it will be necessary to visit a strip club at least once.

11. All telephone numbers in America begin with the digits 555.

12. If being chased through town, you can usually take cover in a passing St. Patrick's Day parade—at any time of the year.

13. All grocery shopping bags contain at least one stick of French bread.

14. Anyone can land a plane, providing there is someone in the control tower to talk him down.

15. Once applied, lipstick will never rub off—even while scuba diving.

16. The ventilation system of any building is the perfect hiding place. No one will ever think of looking for you in there, and you can travel to any other part of the building you want without difficulty.

17. If you need to reload your gun, you will always have more ammunition—even if you haven't been carrying any before now.

18. Talking scarecrows, lions, and great wizards of emerald cities exist, and there is no paperwork involved when your house lands on a witch.

Snarky Descriptions

> She's a vacuum with nipples.[7]

> He looks like a condom filled with walnuts.[8]

> As an actress, her only flair is her nostrils.[9]

> He acts like he's got a Mixmaster up his ass and doesn't want anyone to know it.[10]

> He's the type of man who will end up dying in his own arms.[11]

> Dramatic art, in her opinion, is knowing how to fill a sweater.[12]

> She ran the whole gamut of emotions from A to B.[13]

> He gives her class—she gives him sex.[14]

An actor is a guy who, if you ain't talking about
him, he ain't listening.
—MARLON BRANDO

✦✦✦

[7]   Otto Preminger on Marilyn Monroe
[8]   Clive James on Arnold Schwarzenegger
[9]   Pauline Kael on Candice Bergen
[10] Marlon Brando on Montgomery Clift
[11] Mamie van Doren on Warren Beatty
[12] Bette Davis on Jayne Mansfield
[13] Dorothy Parker on Katharine Hepburn
[14] Katherine Hepburn on Fred Astaire and Ginger Rogers

Stephen Spielberg is so powerful he had final
cut at his own circumcision.
—ROBIN WILLIAMS

✦✦

A wide screen just makes a bad film twice as bad.
—SAMUEL GOLDWYN

✦✦✦

Yes, I shot a few scenes out of focus.
I wanted to win the foreign film award.
—BILLY WILDER

Concession Stand Snark

You're at the concession stand when the two behemoths
in the front of the line can't decide between the
large popcorn or the super-mega-large popcorn,
the ten-pound bag of plain or peanut M&Ms,
the gross of Twizzlers, or the garbage pail of
Milk Duds. The diet soda is a given. Snark time.
Go ahead, let it fly:

➤ "So what? You're feeding an entire African
   country?"

➤ "How many shows are you staying for?"

➤ "Should I ask the usher for a wheelbarrow?"

➤ "Whatever you do, stay away from the beach, Shamu!"

~✦~

Following a woman with a dog out of the movie theater, a man stopped her and said, "I'm sorry to bother you, but I was amazed that your dog seemed to get into the movie so much. He cried at the right spots, moved nervously at the boring spots, and laughed like crazy at the funny parts. Don't you find that unusual?"

"Yes," she replied, "I find it very unusual. Especially considering that he hated the book!"

~✦~

Snarky Movie Descriptions

> *Gone with the Wind:* A movie about a fire, for god's sake.

> *Lawrence of Arabia:* Lots of sand, but no self-respecting gay man would be caught dead wearing what he's got on in most of the movie. Nice uniform, though.

> *Casablanca:* A woman walks into a bar. Should be a snark here. There ain't one. And doesn't that piano player know anything else?

> *Singing in the Rain:* An idiot without sense enough to come in out of the rain sings in the rain and nearly drowns.

> *West Side Story:* The whitest gangs ever who break into song every time they're supposed to fight.

> *Citizen Kane:* Two hours of angst over a sled. A fucking sled.

- *On the Waterfront:* Hey pal . . . no way you would have been a contender. And leave her goddamn gloves alone.

- *The Godfather:* Guy gets pissed. Kills everyone. Even his brother. Kissed him first, though. Nice touch.

- *Annie Hall:* La da dee, la di da. Shut the fuck up. Somebody hit her . . . please? And hard. And Grammy Hall while you're at it.

- *Star Wars:* Let's see: A woman with two sticky buns on her head, a shag carpet, a vacuum cleaner, and a gay robot save the universe. Could happen.

- *The Bicycle Thief:* A kid steals a bike. An old, decrepit, shitty little bike. Yeah, let's go make a movie.

- *High Noon:* Three men come into town to kill a sheriff with no facial expressions or any discernible acting ability.

- *2001: A Space Odyssey:* In space, no one can hear you yawn. Too bad.

- *Midnight Cowboy:* A gigolo from Texas and a homeless man become fast friends. Made during the drug era. Clearly.

- *One Flew Over the Cuckoo's Nest:* Jack Nicholson in the role he would repeat in every movie he made afterward.

- *Good Will Hunting:* A troubled genius with a photographic memory works as a janitor at MIT? Don't troubled geniuses live in the backwoods somewhere building explosive devices to mail to MIT?

Let the Snark Flow: Silver Screen Edition

> *Spinal Tap*: Rob Reiner, son of Carl, honed his chops on *All in the Family*.

> *Duck Soup* or most any Marx Brothers movie: Groucho is the ultimate snarker.

> *The Meaning of Life* or most any Monty Python movie: British snark at its finest.

> *Who's Afraid of Virginia Woolf?*: Liz Taylor and Richard Burton with vintage relationship snark.

> *Some Like It Hot*: Jack Lemmon and Tony Curtis in a dress? Need I say more?

> *Mean Girls*: Tina Fey is the hardest working snarker in show bidness.

> *Dorothy Parker* and *the Round Table*: Talk about talking through a wet tissue . . . but it's the closest we might get to seeing Dorothy Parker in action.

> *Reservoir Dogs* and *Pulp Fiction*: Quentin Tarantino loves the witty bon mot . . . usually covered in blood.

> *Arthur*: Drunks always make for the very best in snark . . . followed closely by butlers.

> *My Favorite Year*: Jews, the early days of TV, a faux Sid Caesar. Good stuff.

> *State and Main* and much of David Mamet's ouevre: William H. Macy riffing every which way.

> *Swingers*: Vince Vaughn at his most obnoxious, especially in the diner at the end.

- ➤ *American Beauty*: Middle-age angst and lust . . . a heady combination.
- ➤ *As Good as It Gets*: Almost as much fun as OCD, gay bashing, and a road trip with Helen Hunt.
- ➤ *The Boys in the Band*: Put twelve snarky gay men in a room and get out of the way.
- ➤ *Closer*: Clive Owens is an up-and-comer in the snark game. The back and forth with Julia Roberts is snark nirvana.

Snarky Dialogue

You know how to whistle, don't you, Steve?
Just put your lips together and blow.
—LAUREN BACALL IN *TO HAVE OR HAVE NOT*

++

Get this big walking carpet out of my way.
—CARRIE FISHER IN *STAR WARS*

+++

Women need a reason to have sex. Men just need a place.
—BILLY CRYSTAL IN *CITY SLICKERS*

++

It's not a lie. I have a gift for fiction.
—WILLIAM H. MACY IN *STATE AND MAIN*

+++

You know, you haven't stopped talking since I came here? You must
have been vaccinated with a phonograph needle.
—GROUCHO MARX IN *DUCK SOUP*

++

Fasten your seatbelts, it's going
to be a bumpy night!
—BETTE DAVIS IN *ALL ABOUT EVE*

+++

Oh, wake up, Norma, you'd be killing yourself to an empty house.
The audience left twenty years ago.
—WILLIAM HOLDEN IN *SUNSET BOULEVARD*

++

Leave the gun. Take the cannoli.
—RICHARD S. CASTELLANO IN *THE GODFATHER*

+++

Television is more interesting than people. If it were not, we would
have people standing in the corners of our rooms.
—ALAN CORENK

++

Television enables you to be entertained in your home by people you
wouldn't have in your home.
—DAVID FROST

+++

Imitation is the sincerest form of television.
—FRED ALLEN

++

Let the Snark Flow: Small Screen Edition

- ➤ *Seinfeld/Curb Your Enthusiasm:* Larry David. 'Nuff said?
- ➤ *30 Rock:* The inimitable Ms. Fey again.
- ➤ *M*A*S*H:* Great writing and Alan Alda, clearly a Groucho fan.
- ➤ *The Daily Show:* Meet Jon Stewart, the reigning king of snark.[15]
- ➤ *The Colbert Report:* Meet Stephen Colbert, the reigning king of snark.[16]
- ➤ *Californication:* More snark in a half hour than most any other show.
- ➤ *24:* Guaranteed snark from Chloe to just about everyone.
- ➤ *Sports Night/West Wing/Studio 60:* Anything from Aaron Sorkin.
- ➤ *Two and a Half Men:* Even with Charlie Sheen and Jon Cryer, this is a great source.
- ➤ *Roseanne:* Made into an art form by Ms. Barr.
- ➤ *Rescue Me:* The art form perfected by Denis Leary.
- ➤ *House:* Curmudgeons also make for the best snarkers.
- ➤ *Arrested Development:* King of the killer asides—the entire show had a snark attitude.

---

[15] Or was that Stephen Colbert?
[16] Or was that Jon Stewart?

The Supreme Court says pornography is anything without artistic
merit that causes sexual thoughts; that's their definition, essentially.
No artistic merit, causes sexual thoughts. Hmm . . . sounds like . . .
every commercial on television, doesn't it?
—BILL HICKS

+++

Television: A medium. So called because it is
neither rare nor well done.
—DAVID LETTERMAN

++

Don't you wish there were a knob on the
TV to turn up the intelligence? There's one
marked *brightness*, but it doesn't work.
—COMEDIAN GALLAGHER

+++

I find television very educating. Every time somebody turns on the set,
I go into the other room and read a book.
—GROUCHO MARX

++

TV commercials now show you how detergents take out bloodstains,
a pretty violent image there. I think if you've got a T-shirt with a
bloodstain all over it, maybe laundry isn't your biggest problem.
—JERRY SEINFELD

+++

~+~

A newspaper reporter was writing a feature story about prison life and was interviewing one of the prisoners. "Do you watch much television here?"

"Only the daytime shows," the inmate said. "At night we're locked in our cells and don't see any television."

"That's too bad," the reporter said, "But I do think it is nice that the warden lets you watch it in the daytime."

"What do you mean, 'nice'?" the inmate said. "That's part of the punishment."

THE BOOK OF
INSULTS

Literature

Nature, not content with denying him the
ability to think, has endowed him with the
ability to write.
—A. E. HOUSMAN

+++

Ordinarily he is insane. But he has lucid moments
when he is only stupid.
—HEINRICH HEINE

++

She and her sex had better mind the kitchen and her children; and
perhaps the poor; except in such things as little novels, they only
devote themselves to what men do much better, leaving that which
men do worse or not at all.
—EDWARD FITZGERALD ON ELIZABETH
BARRETT BROWNING

+++

If a person is not talented enough to be a novelist, not smart enough to be a lawyer, and his hands are too shaky to perform operations, he becomes a journalist.
—NORMAN MAILER

♦♦

Everywhere I go I'm asked if I think the university stifles writers. My opinion is that they don't stifle enough of them.
—FLANNERY O'CONNOR

♦♦♦

Any reviewer who expresses rage and loathing for a novel is preposterous. He or she is like a person who has put on full armor and attacked a hot fudge sundae.[17]
—KURT VONNEGUT

~♦~

Edna Ferber, one of the brightest lights in the New York "Algonquin Round Table Group" of the twenties and thirties, had a penchant for wearing elegantly tailored suits, trousers and all. Noël Coward met her one day in New York when he was wearing a suit very similar to the one Miss Ferber was sporting. "Edna, you look almost like a man," he told her. "So do you," she answered.

~♦~

---

[17] Hey Kurt, relax. If Attila the Hun were alive today, he'd be a critic.

He is the same old sausage, fizzing and
sputtering in his own grease.
—HENRY JAMES

✦✦

You're a mouse studying to be a rat.
—WILSON MIZNER

✦✦✦

Mr. Huxley is perhaps one of
those people who have to perpetrate thirty bad novels before
producing a good one.
—T. S. ELIOT ON ALDOUS HUXLEY

✦✦

He knows so little and knows it so fluently.
—ELLEN GLASGOW

✦✦✦

He looked as inconspicuous as a tarantula on a
slice of angel food.
—RAYMOND CHANDLER

✦✦

Match the Criticism to the Book[18]

A. *Paradise Lost*
   (John Milton)
B. *Three Lives*
   (Gertrude Stein)
C. *Moby-Dick*
   (Herman Melville)

D. *Uncle Tom's Cabin*
   (Harriet Beecher Stowe)
E. *Franny and Zooey*
   (J. D. Salinger)
F. *A Man in Full*
   (Tom Wolfe)

~•~

1. Nobody can be more clownish, more clumsy and sententiously in bad taste . . . Oh dear, when the solemn ass brays! brays! brays! —D. H. Lawrence

2. A cold suet-roll of fabulously reptilian length. Cut it at any point, it is the same thing; the same heavy, sticky, opaque mass all through and all along. —Wyndham Lewis

3. The book has gas and runs out of gas, fills up again, goes dry. It is a 742-page work that reads as if it is fifteen hundred pages long. . . . —Norman Mailer

4. One of the books which the reader admires and lays down, and forgets to take up again. None ever wished it longer than it is. —Samuel Johnson

5. So you're the little woman who wrote the book that made this great war. —Abraham Lincoln

6. It suffers from this terrible sort of metropolitan sentimentality and it's so narcissistic . . . so false, so calculated. Combining the plain

---

[18] 1. C, 2. B, 3. F, 4. A, 5. D, 6. E

man with an absolutely megalomaniac egotism. I simply can't stand
it. —Mary McCarthy

We do not have to visit a madhouse to
find disordered minds; our planet is the mental institution of the
universe.
JOHANN WOLFGANG VON GOETHE

+++

A flabby lemon and pink giant, who hung his mouth open as though
he were an animal at the zoo inviting buns—especially when the
ladies were present.
—WYNDHAM LEWIS ON FORD MADOX FORD

++

A book by Henry James is like a church lit but without a congregation
to distract you, with every light and line focused on the high altar.
And on the altar, very reverently placed, intensely there, is a dead
kitten, an eggshell, a bit of string.
—H. G. WELLS

+++

Dorothy Parker

↪ That woman speaks eighteen languages and can't say no in any of them.

↪ She looks like something that would eat its young. (On Dame Edith Evans)

↪ The affair between Margot Asquith and Margot Asquith will live as one of the prettiest love stories in all literature.

A louse in the locks of literature.
—LORD ALFRED TENNYSON
ON CRITIC CHURTON COLLINS

••

He is a bad novelist and a fool. The combination usually makes for great popularity in the US.
—GORE VIDAL ON ALEKSANDR SOLZHENITSYN

•••

He missed an invaluable opportunity to hold his tongue.
—ANDREW LANG

••

He was born stupid, and greatly increased his birthright.
—SAMUEL BUTLER

•••

He was one of those men who possess almost every gift, except the gift of the power to use them.
—CHARLES KINGSLEY

••

Insults and More Insults

↝ He walked as if he had fouled his small clothes and looks as if he smelt it.[19]

↝ Mr. Eliot is at times an excellent poet and has arrived at the supreme Eminence among English critics largely through disguising himself as a corpse.[20]

↝ He was humane but not human.[21]

↝ He had a mind so fine that no idea could violate it.[22]

↝ I don't think Robert Browning was very good in bed. His wife probably didn't care for him very much. He snored and had fantasies about twelve-year-old girls.[23]

↝ Gibbon's style is detestable; but it is not the worst thing about him.[24]

↝ An unmanly sort of man whose love-life seems to have been largely confined to crying in laps and playing mouse.[25]

↝ In conversation he is even duller than in writing, if that is possible.[26]

---

[19] Christopher Smart on Thomas Gray
[20] Ezra Pound on T. S. Eliot
[21] E. E. Cummings on Ezra Pound
[22] T. S. Eliot on Henry James
[23] W. H. Auden on Robert Browning
[24] Samuel Taylor Coleridge on Edward Gibbon
[25] W. H. Auden on Edgar Allan Poe
[26] Juliana Smith on Noah Webster

While he was not dumber than an ox he
was not any smarter either.
—JAMES THURBER

✦✦✦

He is not only dull himself, he is the cause of
dullness in others.
—SAMUEL JOHNSON

✦✦

He is one of those people who would be enormously improved by
death.
—H. H. MUNRO

✦✦✦

Nature played a cruel trick on her by giving
her a waxed mustache.
—ALAN BENNETT

✦✦

Some folks are wise and some are otherwise.
—TOBIAS GEORGE SMOLLETT

✦✦✦

Some folks seem to have descended from the chimpanzee later than
others.
—KIN HUBBARD

✦✦

That's not writing; that's typing.[27]
—TRUMAN CAPOTE ON JACK KEROUAC

~♦~

Clark Gable to William Faulkner: "Oh, Mr. Faulkner, do you write?" William Faulkner to Clark Gable: "Yes, I do, Mr. Gable. What do you do?"

~♦~

His mind is so open that the wind whistles through it.
—HEYWOOD BROUN

♦♦♦

He must have had a magnificent build before his stomach went in for a career of its own.
—MARGARET HALSEY

♦♦

I've just learned about his illness.
Let's hope it's nothing trivial.
—IRVIN S. COBB

♦♦♦

He not only overflowed with learning,
but stood in the slop.
—SYDNEY SMITH

♦♦

---

[27] This is ridiculous. Everyone knows you can't type on toilet paper.

He was a solemn, unsmiling, sanctimonious
old iceberg who looked like he was waiting
for a vacancy in the Trilogy.
—MARK TWAIN

✦✦✦

His style has the desperate jauntiness of an orchestra fiddling away
for dear life on a sinking ship.
—EDMUND WILSON ON EVELYN WAUGH

✦✦

His features resembled a fossilized washrag.
—ALAN BRIEN

✦✦✦

His ignorance covers the world like a blanket, and there's scarcely a
hole in it anywhere.
—MARK TWAIN

✦✦

She's the triumph of sugar over diabetes.
—GEORGE JEAN NATHAN

✦✦✦

His face was filled with broken commandments.
—JOHN MASEFIELD

✦✦

Snarkin' the News

↬ HarperCollins is paying Scott Brown a lot of money to bare all in his memoirs. What happened to the days when you actually had to do something first to get a book deal? He'll have to wait and read his own book to find out what it is he's actually done.

↬ Other news: A judge ordered a website to remove a fictional story about a berserk giraffe that attacked a guide at a local zoo . . . perhaps because it was too hard to swallow?

↬ A copy of a *Superman #1* comic book sold recently for $1 million and nerds all over America could be heard yelling at their mothers for throwing their copies away when they cleaned out the basement.

She was what we used to call a
suicide blonde—dyed by her own hand.
—SAUL BELLOW

+++

Insults and More Insults

- He was a great friend of mine. Well, as much as you could be a friend of his, unless you were a fourteen-year-old nymphet.[28]
- A little emasculated mass of inanity.[29]
- He's a full-fledged housewife from Kansas with all the prejudices.[30]
- I am reading Henry James . . . and feel myself as one entombed in a block of smooth amber.[31]
- In her last days, she resembled a spoiled pear.[32]
- He is always willing to lend a helping hand to the ones above him. [33]
- I am fairly unrepentant about her poetry. I really think that three quarters of it is gibberish. However, I must crush down these thoughts; otherwise the dove of peace will shit on me.[34]

---

28 Truman Capote on William Faulkner
29 Theodore Roosevelt on Henry James
30 Gore Vidal on Truman Capote
31 Virginia Woolf on Henry James
32 Gore Vidal on Gertrude Stein
33 F. Scott Fitzgerald about Ernest Hemingway
34 Noël Coward on Edith Sitwell

Match the Insult to the Book[35]

A. *The Idiot*
   (Fyodor Dostoevsky)

B. *Pride and Prejudice*
   (Jane Austen)

C. *Skinny Bitch*
   (Freedman and
   Barnouin)

D. *Lullaby*
   (Chuck Palahniuk)

E. *Harry Potter and the
   Prisoner of Azkaban*
   (J. K. Rowling)

F. *Fear and Loathing in
   Las Vegas*
   (Hunter Thompson)

~•~

1. You foul, loathsome, evil little cockroach.
2. You have delighted us long enough.
3. Maybe humans are just the pet alligators that God flushed down the toilet.
4. I hate you . . . you are the type, the incarnation, the acme of the most insolent and self-satisfied, the most vulgar and loathsome commonplaceness. Yours is the commonplaceness of pomposity, of self-satisfaction and olympian serenity. You are the most ordinary of the ordinary!
5. Is that a beard, or are you eating a muskrat?
6. Coffee is for pussies.

---

[35] 1. E, 2. B, 3. D, 4. A, 5. F, 6. C

She's the sort of woman who lives for others—you can tell the others
by their hunted expression.
—C. S. LEWIS

✦✦

I worship the quicksand he walks in.
—ART BUCHWALD

~✦~

When Dorothy Parker was told that Calvin Coolidge
had died, she asked: "How can they tell?"

~✦~

She could carry off anything; and
some people said that she did.
—ADA LEVERSON

✦✦✦

They hardly make 'em like him any more—but just to be on the safe
side, he should be castrated anyway.
—HUNTER S. THOMPSON

✦✦

He's as useless as a pulled tooth.
—MARY ROBERTS RINEHART

✦✦✦

He never chooses an opinion; he
just wears whatever happens to be in style.
—LEO TOLSTOY

✦✦

Oscar Wilde

- ↝ There are two ways of disliking poetry; one way is to dislike it, the other is to read Pope.

- ↝ He has no enemies, but is intensely disliked by his friends.

- ↝ Some cause happiness wherever they go; others whenever they go.

- ↝ Fashion is what one wears oneself. What is unfashionable is what other people wear.

- ↝ When the gods wish to punish us they answer our prayers.

- ↝ I don't recognize you—I've changed a lot.

- ↝ Only dull people are brilliant at breakfast.

- ↝ One should always be in love. This is the reason one should never marry.

- ↝ Fashion is a form of ugliness so intolerable that we have to alter it every six months.

- ↝ She is a peacock in everything but beauty.

- ↝ He hadn't a single redeeming vice.

- ↝ He has one of those characteristic British faces that, once seen, are never remembered.

- ↝ The play was a great success, but the audience was a disaster.

He was a bit like a corkscrew.
Twisted, cold, and sharp.
—KATE CRUISE O'BRIEN

+++

He's a wit with dunces, and a dunce with wits.
—ALEXANDER POPE

++

He has a brain of feathers, and a heart of lead.
—ALEXANDER POPE

+++

He had delusions of adequacy.
—WALTER KERR

++

He was one of the nicest old ladies I ever met.
—WILLIAM FAULKNER

+++

The ineffable dunce has nothing to say and says it with a liberal embellishment of bad delivery, embroidering it with reasonless vulgarities of attitude, gesture, and attire. There never was an impostor so hateful, a blockhead so stupid, a crank so variously and offensively daft. He makes me tired.
—AMBROSE BIERCE ON OSCAR WILDE

++

I want to reach your mind—where is it currently located?
—ASHLEIGH BRILLIANT

+++

Why don't you get a haircut?
You look like a chrysanthemum.
—P. G. WODEHOUSE

She was a large woman who seemed
not so much dressed as upholstered.[36]
—JAMES MATTHEW BARRIE

Full Circle (ish) Snark

↔ **Sir Walter Scott, according to Mark Twain**

He did measureless harm; more real and lasting harm, perhaps, than any other individual that ever wrote.

↔ **Mark Twain, according to William Faulkner**

A hack writer who would not have been considered fourth rate in Europe, who tricked out a few of the old proven "sure-fire" literary skeletons with sufficient local color to intrigue the superficial and the lazy.

↔ **William Faulkner, according to Ernest Hemingway**

Have you ever heard of anyone who drank while he worked? You're thinking of Faulkner. He does sometimes—and I can tell right in the middle of a page when he's had his first one.

↔ **Ernest Hemingway, according to Vladimir Nabokov**

I read him for the first time in the early forties, something about bells, balls, and bulls, and loathed it.

---

[36] This from the guy who wrote *Peter Pan?*

Catfight

↔ **Tom Wolfe, according to John Irving**

You see people reading him on airplanes, the same people who are reading John Grisham, for Christ's sake . . . I'm using the argument against him that he can't write, that his sentences are bad, that it makes you wince. You know, if you were a good skater, could you watch someone just fall down all the time? Could you do that? I can't do that.

↔ **Tom Wolfe, according to Norman Mailer**

At certain points, reading [*A Man in Full*] can even be said to resemble the act of making love to a three-hundred-pound woman. Once she gets on top, it's over. Fall in love, or be asphyxiated.

↔ **Tom Wolfe, according to John Updike**

A Man in Full still amounts to entertainment, not literature, even literature in a modest aspirant form. Like a movie desperate to recoup its bankers' investment, the novel tries too hard to please us.

↔ **John Irving, Norman Mailer, and John Updike, according to Tom Wolfe**

Larry, Curly, and Moe. Updike, Mailer, and Irving. My three stooges. . . . *A Man in Full* had frightened them. They were shaken. It was as simple as that. *A Man in Full* was an example . . . of the likely new direction: the intensely realistic novel . . . a revolution in content rather than form . . . that was about to sweep the arts in America, a revolution that would soon make many prestigious artists, such as our three old novelists, appear effete and irrelevant.

I will always love the false image I had of you.
—ASHLEIGH BRILLIANT

+++

She's so boring you fall asleep halfway through her name.
—ALAN BENNETT

++

She has been kissed as often as a police-court Bible, and by much the
same class of people.
—ROBERTSON DAVIES

+++

Her skin was white as leprosy.
—S. T. COLERIDGE

++

He was about as useful in a crisis as a sheep.
—DOROTHY EDEN

+++

I could never learn to like her, except on a raft at sea with no other
provisions in sight.
—MARK TWAIN

++

That young girl is one of the least benightedly
unintelligent organic life forms it has been my
profound lack of pleasure not to be able to
avoid meeting.
—DOUGLAS ADAMS

♦♦♦

She looked like a huge ball of fur on two
well-developed legs.
—NANCY MITFORD

♦♦

He was so crooked, you could have
used his spine for a safety-pin.
—DOROTHY L. SAYERS

♦♦♦

He is mad, bad, and dangerous to know.
—LADY CAROLINE LAMB

♦♦

She wears her clothes as if they
were thrown on with a pitchfork.
—JONATHAN SWIFT

♦♦♦

~•~

Dorothy Parker was invited to a party where most of the other guests looked as if they had stepped straight out of a church-hall production of La Bohème. "Where on earth do all these people come from?" her companion asked. "I think that after it's all over they crawl back into the woodwork," she replied.

~•~

She resembles the Venus de Milo: she is very old, has no teeth, and has white spots on her yellow skin.
—HEINRICH HEINE

••

Some people can stay longer in an hour than others can in a week.
—WILLIAM DEAN HOWELLS

•••

She not only expects the worst, but makes the worst of it when it happens.
—MICHAEL ARLEN

••

Failure has gone to his head.
—WILSON MIZNER

+++

He is so mean, he won't let his little baby have
more than one measle at a time.
—EUGENE FIELD

++

Charles Lamb I sincerely believe to be in some considerable degree
insane. A more pitiful, rickety, gasping, staggering, stammering
tomfool I do not know. He is witty by denying truisms and abjuring
good manners. His speech wriggles hither and thither with an
incessant painful fluctuation; not an opinion in it or a fact or
even a phrase that you can thank him for. . . .
—THOMAS CARLYLE

+++

Bret Harte is a liar, a thief, a swindler, a snob, a sot, a sponge, a
coward, a Jeremy Diddler, he is brim full of treachery, and he conceals
his Jewish birth as carefully as if he considered it a disgrace.
—MARK TWAIN

++

Snarky Criticism

↔ An enthusiasm for Poe is the mark of a decidedly primitive stage of reflection.[37]

↔ Isn't she a poisonous thing of a woman, lying, concealing, flipping, plagiarising, misquoting, and being as clever a crooked literary publicist as ever?[38]

↔ I am reading Proust for the first time. Very poor stuff. I think he was mentally defective.[39]

↔ Every time I read *Pride and Prejudice*, I want to dig [Jane Austen] up and hit her over the skull with her own shin-bone.[40]

↔ E. M. Forster never gets any further than warming the teapot. He's a rare fine hand at that. Feel this teapot. Is it not beautifully warm? Yes, but there ain't going to be no tea.[41]

↔ I can't read ten pages of Steinbeck without throwing up.[42]

↔ His work is evil, and he is one of those unhappy beings of whom one can say that it would be better had he never been born.[43]

↔ A more sententious, holding-forth old bore, who expected every hero-worshipping adenoidal little twerp of a student-poet to hang on his every word I never saw.[44]

---

[37] Henry James on Edgar Allen Poe
[38] Dylan Thomas on Edith Sitwell
[39] Evelyn Waugh on Marcel Proust
[40] Mark Twain on Jane Austen
[41] Katherine Mansfield on E. M. Forster
[42] James Gould Cozzens on John Steinbeck
[43] Anatole France on Émile Zola
[44] James Dickey on Robert Frost

I regard you with an indifference
bordering on aversion.
—ROBERT LOUIS STEVENSON

✦✦✦

She never lets ideas interrupt the easy flow of her conversation.
—JEAN WEBSTER

✦✦

God was bored by him.
—VICTOR HUGO

✦✦✦

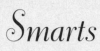

Smarts

SMARTS

OR LACK THEREOF

I'm exhausted. Knowing everything is hard work, and even though I kind of get off on maintaining my IQ while my fellow humans seem to be getting dumber than ever before, it's enough to make me take to my bed. Thank God you have this book in your hands—otherwise you might be tuning out to some idiotic reality television show or cruising porn on the 'Net. What's that? You want to jump in and say something? Here's some advice: Refrain from Twittering something that seems intellectual when you clearly don't know what you're talking about. If someone else's opinion is out there before yours . . . well, is that really so bad? Keep reading, pal. That's the only way to exercise your mind. You can be the sharpest knife in the drawer.[1]

The twinkle in his eyes is actually the sun shining between his ears.

✦

I'm sorry, how many times did your parents drop you when you were a baby?

✦

You're changing your mind? And you think the new one will be any better?

✦

I am so clever sometimes I don't understand a single word of what I'm saying.

✦

Instant idiot. Just add alcohol.

✦

I'm sarcastic because it's the body's natural defense against stupid.

✦

He's about as useless as the pope's testicles.

[1] Just remember that I'm a razor in comparison.

He's so stupid he got hit by a parked car.

✦

Does this rag smell like chloroform to you?

✦

You'd think such a little mind would be lonely in such a big head.

✦

If ignorance is bliss, you must be the happiest person alive.

✦

She doesn't know the meaning of the word "fear," but then again, she doesn't know the meaning of most words.

The IQ and the life expectancy of the average man recently passed each other in opposite directions.

How do you keep an idiot in suspense? Leave a message and I'll get back to you.

✦

Some people drink from the fountain of knowledge—it appears that you just gargled.

Don't hesitate to speak your mind . . . you have nothing to lose.

Beauty

BEAUTY

(OR LACK THEREOF)

You know that not particularly clever phrase "coyote ugly"? Meaning that you wake up with the person you met in the bar last night when you were so drunk that you actually thought you looked good in the bathroom mirror[1] and this person is laying on your arm and you'd almost rather chew it off than wake them . . . you don't want to get there. I realize that looks are subjective . . . just please don't subject me to the bad ones. I've heard some wise men claim that confidence makes up for ugliness, but I dunno, it doesn't work for me. Makeup can go a ways to help, and being generous sexually is always a good remedy—some faces look a lot better from the top of the head down. Be careful, though . . . it's actually harder to run with just one arm.

Do you think that I'll lose my looks when I get older? With luck, yes . . .

+

Roses are red, violets are blue, God made me pretty; what the hell happened to you?

You used to look your age; now, you don't even look your species.

+

Your hairdresser must really hate you.

+

He has the face of a saint—a Saint Bernard.

Hit with the ugly stick? You must have been born in the ugly forest. Looks like you fell out of the ugly tree and hit every branch on the way down.

---

[1] Even though the shiny part had actually peeled off.

When you come into a room, the mice jump on chairs.

Well, obviously this day was a total waste of makeup.

I always say that the best years of a woman's life are the ten years between thirty and thirty-one.

You're lucky to be born beautiful; unlike me, who was born a huge liar.

That woman's had her face lifted so many times there's nothing left inside her shoes.

You look like you comb your hair with an eggbeater.

See, that's what's meant by dark and handsome. When it's dark, he's handsome.

Don't hate me because I'm beautiful . . . hate me because your boyfriend thinks I'm beautiful.

Sports

Baseball without fans is like Jayne Mansfield without a sweater. Hang on, that can be taken two ways.
—RICHARD NIXON

~•~

Back in 1961, the Cincinnati Reds had a Venezuelan shortstop named Elio Chacón, whose command of the English language was limited, and a Cuban coach named Reggie Otero with much better bilingual skills. The story is that one day an umpire made a questionable call adverse to Chacón and the Reds and Chacón went into a tirade in Spanish. The umpire asked Otero, "Did he just call me what I think he called me?" and Otero replied, "Oh no, he doesn't know enough English to call you what you are," and with that the umpire threw Otero out of the game.

~•~

Bruce Benedict is so slow he'd finish third in a race with a pregnant woman.
—TOMMY LASORDA

+++

If you think it's hard to meet new people, try picking up the wrong golf ball.
—JACK LEMMON

++

Terry Bradshaw is so dumb, he couldn't spell C–A–T if you spotted him the C and the A.
—THOMAS HENDERSON

~+~

Shelby Metcalf, basketball coach at Texas A&M, re-counting what he told a player who received four Fs and one D: "Son, looks to me like you're spending too much time on one subject."

~+~

Dick Cheney's defense is that he was aiming at a quail when he shot the guy. Which means that Cheney now has the worst aim of anyone in the White House since Bill Clinton.
—JAY LENO, COMMENTING ON THE VICE PRESIDENT'S HUNTING MISHAP WHEN HE SHOT HIS FRIEND INSTEAD OF A BIRD

~+~

What has four legs and no ears?
Mike Tyson's dog.

~+~

Match the Insult to the Athlete[45]

A. Muhammad Ali   D. George Best

B. Torii Hunter   E. Maria Sharapova

C. Roy Keane   F. John McEnroe

1. You were a crap player, you are a crap manager. The only reason I have any dealings with you is that somehow you are manager of my country and you're not even Irish, you English ****. You can stick it up your bollocks.
2. I'm not the next [Anna] Kournikova—I want to win matches.
3. Joe Frazier is so ugly he should donate his face to the US Bureau of Wildlife.
4. What problems do you have, apart from being unemployed, a moron, and a dork?
5. He cannot kick with his left foot, he cannot head a ball, he cannot tackle, and he doesn't score many goals. Apart from that he's all right.
6. Why should I get this kid from the South Side of Chicago and have Scott Boras represent him and pay him $5 million when you can get a Dominican guy for a bag of chips?

---

[45] 1. C, 2. E, 3. A, 4. F, 5. D, 6. B

Putting allows the touchy golfer two to four opportunities to blow a gasket in the short space of two to forty feet.
—TOMMY BOLT

++

What's the difference between a three-week-old puppy and a sportswriter? In six weeks, the puppy stops whining.
—MIKE DITKA

+++

What's the penalty for killing a photographer?
One stroke or two?
—PRO GOLFER DAVIS LOVE III

++

Golf and sex are about the only things you can enjoy without being good at them.
—JIMMY DEMARET

+++

Golf is like chasing a quinine pill around a cow pasture.
—WINSTON CHURCHILL

++

I'm tired of hearing about money, money, money, money, money. I just want to play the game, drink Pepsi, and wear Reebok.
—SHAQUILLE O'NEAL

~•~

Sammy Davis was playing golf when the pro asked him his handicap. He replied, "I'm blind in one eye and a Jew."

~•~

The people who gave us golf and called it a game are the same people who gave us bagpipes and called it music.
—ANONYMOUS

•••

As a boxer, he floats like a butterfly
and stings like one, too.
—ANONYMOUS

••

I would like to thank the press from the heart
of my bottom.
—NICK FALDO AFTER WINNING THE 1992 OPEN

•••

I'm not saying my golf game went bad, but if I grew tomatoes, they'd
come up sliced.
—LEE TREVINO

••

Mr. Agnew, I believe you have a slight swing in your flaw.
—JIMMY DEMARET TO SPIRO T. AGNEW

~♦~

Boxing promoter Dan Duva on Mike Tyson going to prison: "Why would anyone expect him to come out smarter? He went to prison for three years, not Princeton."[46]

~♦~

Reporter to George Foreman after 1994 win against Michael Moorer: "Was the fight fixed?" Foreman's response: "Sure the fight was fixed. I fixed it with a right hand."

~♦~

Stu Grimson, Chicago Blackhawks left wing, explaining why he keeps a color photo of himself above his locker: "That's so when I forget how to spell my name, I can still find my clothes."

~♦~

Lou Duva, veteran boxing trainer, on the spartan training regime of heavyweight Andrew Golota: "He's a guy who gets up at six o'clock in the morning, regardless of what time it is."

~♦~

---

[46] Clearly a man with a death wish but the newer, gentler Mike would at least do it fast.

~+~

A man staggers into an emergency room with a concussion, multiple bruises, two black eyes, and a five iron wrapped tightly around his throat. Naturally, the doctor asks him what happened.

"Well, it was like this . . . I was having a quiet round of golf with my wife, when at a difficult hole we both sliced our balls into a pasture of cows. We went to look for them, and while I was rooting around, noticed one of the cows had something white at its rear end. I walked over and lifted up the tail, and sure enough, there was a golf ball with my wife's monogram on it, stuck right in the middle of the cow's butt, and that's when I made my mistake . . ."

"What did you do?" the doctor asked.

"I lifted the cow's tail again and yelled to my wife, 'Hey, this looks like yours!' . . . I don't remember much after that."

~+~

Without the use of drugs our athletes are like drivers
of a racing car with one gear less than their rivals.
—HARVEY SMITH

Insults and More Insults

↔ If they can make penicillin out of moldy bread, they can sure make something out of you.[47]

↔ "My wife just had a baby." "Congratulations! Whose is it?"[48]

↔ Like an octopus falling out of a tree.[49]

↔ Lie down so I can recognize you.[50]

↔ He has so many hooks in his nose, he looks like a piece of bait.[51]

↔ She was so far in the closet she was in danger of being a garment bag.[52]

---

[47] Muhammad Ali to a young boxer
[48] Joe Frazier to Ken Norton
[49] David Feherty, the Irish former golfer, on Jim Furyk's swing
[50] Willie Pep, the American featherweight boxer, when asked by an old opponent if he remembered him
[51] Bob Costas about Dennis Rodman
[52] Rita Mae Brown about Martina Navratilova

Snarkin' the News

↔ Ain't sports grand? The general managers of all of the NHL hockey teams convened this week to decide which hits to the head would be deemed "illegal." Sort of conjures up one big Three Stooges convention, no? "Hey, Moe, pick two fingers. . . ."

↔ The leadoff batter for the Minnesota Twins hit a foul ball into the stands and struck his mother. He will spend the rest of the season in his room.

↔ Tiger Woods dropped out of the TPC because of a "bulge" in his neck. Wasn't a bulge what got him in trouble in the first place?

Torrin Polk, University of Houston receiver, on his coach, John Jenkins: "He treats us like men. He lets us wear earrings."

Football commentator and former player Joe Theismann: "Nobody in football should be called a genius. A genius is a guy like Norman Einstein."

Senior basketball player at the University of Pittsburgh: "I'm going to graduate on time, no matter how long it takes."

~•~

The Dodgers and Giants were playing in 1965, and Lou Johnson lined a ball into the seats down the left-field line. A blind man would've known it was foul, but third-base ump Augie Donatelli made the call anyway.

When the inning ended, Donatelli happened to look toward the stands where the ball went and saw stadium attendants carrying a woman on a stretcher.

As Junior Gilliam trotted out to play third for the Dodgers, Donatelli asked him, "Did Johnson's foul hit that woman?"

"Nah," Gilliam said. "You called it right, and she fainted."

~•~

Amarillo High School and Oiler coach Bum Phillips, when asked by Bob Costas why he takes his wife on all the road trips, responded: "Because she is too damn ugly to kiss good-bye."

~•~

And, upon hearing Joe Jacoby of the 'Skins say, "I'd run over my own mother to win the Super Bowl," Matt Millen of the Raiders said: "To win, I'd run over Joe's mom, too."

~•~

If you're caught on a golf course during a storm and
are afraid of lightning, hold up a 1-iron. Not even
God can hit a 1-iron.
—LEE TREVINO

+++

These greens are so fast I have to hold my putter over the ball and hit
it with the shadow.
—SAM SNEAD

++

I would like to deny all allegations by Bob Hope that
during my last game of golf, I hit an eagle, a birdie,
an elk, and a moose.
—GERALD FORD

+++

Incompetence should not be confined to one sex.
—BILL RUSSELL ON FEMALES OFFICIATING IN THE NBA

++

Things in Golf That Sound Dirty

1. After eighteen holes, I can barely walk.
2. You really whacked the hell out of that sucker.
3. Mind if I join your threesome?
4. Keep your head down and spread your legs a bit more.
5. Hold up . . . I need to wash my balls first.

You've got one problem—you stand too close
to the ball . . . after you've hit it.
—SAM SNEAD

~•~

A look at the transcript from one Tiger Woods inter-
view:
Q: "Do you look forward to playing golf again?"
A: "I dunno, for some reason eighteen holes feels a little
bit like a letdown."

~•~

Fifty years ago, a hundred white men chasing one black
man across a field was called the Ku Klux Klan.
Today it's called the PGA Tour.
—ANONYMOUS

~•~

Shaquille O'Neal was having trouble with his free-throw
shots. To rattle him, opposing player A. C. Greene, co-
founder of the group Athletes for Abstinence, called out,
"You'll be all right as soon as you get some experience."
Shaq replied, "And you'll be okay as soon as you get some
sex."

~•~

The least thing upsets him on the links.
He missed short putts because of the uproar of butterflies
in the adjoining meadows.
—P. G. WODEHOUSE

Charisma

CHARISMA

OR LACK THEREOF

When you're annoying me, I'll let you know it. I think of it as community service, not as being mean. Because otherwise you'll just keep on doing it—your quirks, peculiarities, mannerisms, and traits, which may be cute to your mom[54] but aren't—and quickly everyone you know will be avoiding you like the swine flu. By nipping it in the bud, I'm preventing you from horrifying the entire world with your lack of style, taste, and personality, hence the "service" aspect of my advice. Don't try to convince yourself that it's me. Listen to what I'm saying and change.

You have an inferiority complex—and it's fully justified.

❖

You're not yourself today. I noticed the improvement immediately.

❖

I'm just trying to imagine you with a personality.

❖

Do you have to leave so soon? I was about to poison the tea.

❖

There are enough people to hate in the world already without you working so hard to give us another.

❖

Jesus loves you, but everyone else thinks you're an asshole.

---

[54]   Maybe when you were a four-year-old . . .

Do you ever wonder what life would be like if you'd had enough oxygen at birth?

♦

Of course I'd like to help you out. Which way did you come in?

♦

You know the drill! You leave a message. . . . and I ignore it!

♦

If you see two people talking and one looks bored, he's the other one.

♦

I'm not mean . . . you're just a sissy.

When I think of all the people I respect the most, you're right there, serving them drinks.

I can't seem to remember your name, but please don't help me.

♦

I don't know what your problem is, but I'll bet it's hard to pronounce.

Of all the people I've met . . . you're certainly one of them.

THE BOOK OF
PARENTING

Motherhood

Mothers are fonder than fathers of their children because they are
more certain they are their own.
—ARISTOTLE

✦✦✦

Nobody loves me but my mother, and she could be jivin' too.
—B. B. KING

✦✦

The most remarkable thing about my mother is that for thirty years
she served the family nothing but leftovers. The original meal has
never been found.
—CALVIN TRILLIN

✦✦✦

Think of stretch marks as pregnancy service stripes.
—JOYCE ARMOR

✦✦

I know how to do anything—I'm a mom.
—ROSEANNE BARR

✦✦✦

Simply having children does not make mothers.
—JOHN G. SHEDD

◆◆

My mother used to say that there are no strangers, only friends you haven't met yet. She's now in a maximum security twilight home in Australia.
—DAME EDNA EVERAGE

◆◆◆

I'm a mother with two small children, so I don't take as much crap as I used to.
—PAMELA ANDERSON

◆◆

My mother never saw the irony in calling me a son-of-a-bitch.
—JACK NICHOLSON

◆◆◆

My mom said the only reason men are alive is for lawn care and vehicle maintenance.
—TIM ALLEN

◆◆

When your mother asks, "Do you want a piece of advice?" it is a mere formality. It doesn't matter if you answer yes or no. You're going to get it anyway.
—ERMA BOMBECK

◆◆◆

A suburban mother's role is to deliver children obstetrically once, and
by car for ever after.
—PETER DE VRIES

++

Being a mother isn't simply a matter of having children. To think that
is as absurd as believing that having a piano makes one a musician.
—SYDNEY HARRIS

+++

The hand that rocks the cradle is the hand that rules the world.
—W. R. WALLACE

++

An ounce of mother is worth a ton of priest.
—SPANISH PROVERB

+++

(24/7) . . . once you sign on to be a mother, that's the only shift they
offer.
—JODI PICOULT

++

When my kids become wild and unruly, I use a nice, safe playpen.
When they're finished, I climb out.
—ERMA BOMBECK

+++

If evolution really works, how come mothers only have
two hands?
—MILTON BERLE

++

Worst Parenting Books of All Time

Last Child in the Woods: Outrunning a Bear

Secrets of the Baby Whisperer: Teaching Your Child to Say, "Huh, What's That Again?"

Our Babies, Ourselves: But Mostly, Ourselves

Confessions of a Slacker Mom: A Lesson in Three Pages

Fatherhood: On Twenty Minutes a Week

There are only two things a child will share willingly: communicable diseases and his mother's age.

—BENJAMIN SPOCK

✦✦✦

The worst feature of a new baby is its mother's singing.

—KIN HUBBARD

✦✦

My mom was a garage sale person, save money. Come on in to the garage sale, you might find a shirt. She'd get in that garage sale and point stuff out to you. There's a good fork for a nickel. Yeah, that's beautiful. It's a little high. If it were three cents I'd snap it up.

—LOUIE ANDERSON

✦✦✦

My mother had morning sickness after I was born.

—RODNEY DANGERFIELD

✦✦

My mother buried three husbands, and two of them were just napping.
—RITA RUDNER

✦✦✦

I can remember the first time I had to go to sleep. Mom said, "Steven, time to go to sleep." I said, "But I don't know how." She said, "It's real easy. Just go down to the end of tired and hang a left." So I went down to the end of tired, and just out of curiosity I hung a right. My mother was there, and she said, "I thought I told you to go to sleep."
—STEVEN WRIGHT

✦✦

My mom was a ventriloquist and she always was throwing her voice. For ten years I thought the dog was telling me to kill my father.
—WENDY LIEBMAN

✦✦✦

It would seem that something which means poverty, disorder, and violence every single day should be avoided entirely. But the desire to beget children is a natural urge.
—PHYLLIS DILLER

✦✦

~✦~

A little boy watched, fascinated, as his mother covered her face in cold cream. "Why do you do that?" he asked. "To make myself beautiful."
When she began to rub it off, the boy asked, "Why are you doing that? Did you give up?"

~✦~

My mom said she learned how to swim. Someone took her out in the lake and threw her off the boat. That's how she learned how to swim. I said, "Mom, they weren't trying to teach you how to swim."
—PAULA POUNDSTONE

✦✦✦

Neurotics build castles in the air; psychotics live in them. My mother cleans them.
—RITA RUDNER

✦✦

My mother never breast-fed me; she told me she only liked me as a friend.
—RODNEY DANGERFIELD

✦✦✦

My mother tried to kill me when I was a baby. She denied it. She said she thought the plastic bag would keep me fresh.
—BOB MONKHOUSE

✦✦

I asked Mom if I was a gifted child. She said they certainly wouldn't have paid for me.
—CALVIN, "CALVIN AND HOBBES"

✦✦✦

If Mama ain't happy, ain't nobody happy.
—FERRELL SIMS

✦✦

The mother-child relationship is paradoxical and, in a sense, tragic. It requires the most intense love on the mother's side, yet this very love must help the child grow away from the mother, and to become fully independent.

—ERICH FROMM

✦✦✦

A mother is not a person to lean on, but a person to make leaning unnecessary.

—DOROTHY CANFIELD FISHER

✦✦

No woman should ever marry a man who hated his mother.

—MARTHA GELLHORN

✦✦✦

Mothers are inscrutable beings to their sons, always.

—A. E. COPPARD

✦✦

You know, Moe, my mom once said something that really stuck with me. She said, "Homer, you're a big disappointment," and God bless her soul, she was really onto something.

—HOMER SIMPSON, *THE SIMPSONS*

✦✦✦

My mother's menu consisted of two choices:
Take it or leave it.

—BUDDY HACKETT

✦✦

What my mother believed about cooking is that if you worked hard
and prospered, someone else would
do it for you.
—NORA EPHRON

✦✦✦

My mother is such a lousy cook that Thanksgiving at her house is a
time of sorrow.
—RITA RUDNER

✦✦

My mother was a terrible cook. When I was a child I went ice fishing.
I came back with forty pounds of ice. My mother fried it and we
almost drowned.
—ANONYMOUS

✦✦✦

My mother had a great deal of trouble with me, but I think she
enjoyed it.
—MARK TWAIN

✦✦

My mother loved children—she would have given anything if I had
been one.
—GROUCHO MARX

✦✦✦

The phrase "working mother" is redundant.
—JANE SELLMAN

✦✦

Being a working mom is not easy. You have to be willing to screw up
at every level.
—JAMI GERTZ

+++

Working mothers are guinea pigs in a scientific experiment to show
that sleep is not necessary to human life.
—ANONYMOUS

++

Republicans understand the importance of bondage between a
mother and child.
—DAN QUAYLE

+++

A mother is a person who, seeing there are only four pieces of pie for
five people, promptly announces she never did
care for pie.
—TENNEVA JORDAN

++

All women become like their mothers. That is their tragedy. No man
does. That's his.
—OSCAR WILDE

+++

The heart of a mother is a deep abyss at the bottom of which you will
always find forgiveness.
—HONORÉ DE BALZAC

++

Good moms let you lick the beaters . . . great moms
turn them off first.
—ANONYMOUS

+++

No matter how old a mother is, she watches her middle-aged children
for signs of improvement.
—FLORIDA SCOTT-MAXWELL

++

I want to have children, but my friends scare me. One told me she was
in labor for thirty-six hours. I don't even want to do anything that
feels good for thirty-six hours.
—RITA RUDNER

+++

A vacation means that the family goes away for a rest, accompanied by
mother, who sees that the others get it.
—MARCELENE COX

++

The joys of motherhood are never fully experienced until
the kids are in bed.
—ANONYMOUS

+++

If you have children, the demands made upon you in the first hour of
the morning can make the job of air traffic controller seem like a walk
in the park.
—ANONYMOUS

++

She never quite leaves her children at home, even when she doesn't take them along.
—MARGARET CULKIN BANNING

+++

When you are a mother, you are never really alone in your thoughts. A mother always has to think twice: once for herself, and once for her child.
—SOPHIA LOREN

++

Motherhood has a very humanizing effect. Everything gets reduced to essentials.
—MERYL STREEP

+++

A mother's happiness is like a beacon, lighting up the future but reflected also on the past in the guise of fond memories.
HONORÉ DE BALZAC

++

With what price we pay for the glory of motherhood.
—ISADORA DUNCAN

+++

Youth fades; love droops; the leaves of friendship fall;
a mother's secret hope outlives them all.
—OLIVER WENDELL HOLMES

++

Whatever else is unsure in this stinking dunghill of a world, a mother's love is not.
—JAMES JOYCE

✦✦✦

By and large, mothers and housewives are the only workers who do not have regular time off. They are the great vacation-less class.
—ANNE MORROW LINDBERGH

✦✦

Whenever I'm with my mother, I feel as though I have to spend the whole time avoiding land mines.
—AMY TAN

✦✦✦

There was never a child so lovely but his mother was glad to get him to sleep.
—RALPH WALDO EMERSON

✦✦

Thanks to my mother, not a single cardboard box has found its way back into society. We receive gifts in boxes from stores that went out of business twenty years ago.
—ERMA BOMBECK

✦✦✦

Sweater, n.: garment worn by child when its mother is feeling chilly.
—AMBROSE BIERCE

✦✦

As I have discovered by examining my past, I started out as a child. Coincidentally, so did my brother. My mother did not put all her eggs in one basket, so to speak: She gave me a younger brother named Russell, who taught me what was meant by "survival of the fittest."
—BILL COSBY

+++

Somewhere on this globe, every ten seconds, there is a woman giving birth to a child. She must be found and stopped.
—SAM LEVENSON

++

Never lend your car to anyone to whom you have given birth.
—ERMA BOMBECK

++

Your sons weren't made to like you. That's what grandchildren are for.
—JANE SMILEY

++

When my husband comes home, if the kids are still alive, I figure I've done my job.
—ROSEANNE BARR

+++

Top 10 Things Mothers Are Responsible for:

1. Cooking
2. Cleaning
3. Discipline
4. Homework
5. Shopping
6. Transportation
7. Playdates
8. Scheduling
9. Holidays
10. Finding peace in the Middle East

I ask people why they have deer heads on their walls. They always say because it's such a beautiful animal. There you go. I think my mother is attractive, but I have photographs of her.

—ELLEN DEGENERES

~•~

A woman was walking down the street with her blouse open. A passerby stopped and said, "Excuse me, Madam, but your breast is hanging out." She looked down and shrieked, "Oh my god, I left my baby on the bus!"

~•~

If there were no schools to take the children away from home part of the time, the insane asylums would be filled with mothers.

—EDWARD W. HOWE

••

Mother is far too clever to understand anything she does not like.

—ARNOLD BENNETT

•••

Fatherhood

I have good kids. I'm trying to bring them up the right way, not
spanking them. I find waving the gun around
gets the same job done.
—DENIS LEARY

+++

You wake up one day and say, "I don't think I ever need to sleep or
have sex again." Congratulations, you're ready
to have children.
—RAY ROMANO

++

There are no perfect parents. Even Jesus had a distant father and a
domineering mother. I'd have trust issues if my father allowed me to
be crucified.
—BOB SMITH

+++

If the new American father feels bewildered and even defeated, let
him take comfort from the fact that whatever he does in any fathering
situation has a fifty percent chance of being right.
—BILL COSBY

++

I've got seven kids. The three words you hear most around my house are: hello, good-bye, and I'm pregnant.
—DEAN MARTIN

✦✦✦

No man is responsible for his father. That was entirely
his mother's affair.
—MARGARET TURNBULL

✦✦

To be a successful father there's one absolute rule: When you have a kid, don't look at it for the first two years.
—ERNEST HEMINGWAY

✦✦✦

I want my kids to have the things in life that I never had when I was growing up. Things like beards and chest hair.
—JAROD KINTZ

✦✦

Fatherhood is pretending the present you love most
is soap-on-a-rope.
—BILL COSBY

✦✦✦

That is the thankless position of the father in the family: The provider for all and the enemy of all.
—J. AUGUST STRINDBERG

✦✦

By the time a man realizes that maybe his father was right, he usually
has a son who thinks he's wrong.

—CHARLES WADSWORTH

+++

When I was a boy of fourteen, my father was so ignorant I could
hardly stand to have the old man around. But when I got to be
twenty-one, I was astonished at how much the old man had learned in
seven years.

—MARK TWAIN

++

The thing to remember about fathers is . . . they're men. A girl has
to keep it in mind: They are dragon-seekers, bent on improbable
rescues. Scratch any father, you find someone chock-full of qualms
and romantic terrors, believing change is a threat, like your first shoes
with heels on, like your first bicycle . . .

—PHYLLIS McGINLEY

~+~

Dad had once said, "Trust your mind, Rob. If it smells like
shit but has writing across it that says 'Happy Birthday'
and a candle stuck down in it, what is it?"

"Is there icing on it?" I'd said.

Dad had done that thing of squinting his eyes when
an answer was not quite there yet.

—GEORGE SAUNDERS

~+~

More of the Worst Parenting Books of All Time

Siblings Without Rivalry: Keeping Separate Households in Different States
The Happiest Toddler on the Block: The Joys of Ritalin
The No-Cry Sleep Solution by Jack Daniels
The Baby Bond: 50 Shades of Spit-Up

Sir Walter, being strangely surprised and put out of his countenance at so great a table, gives his son a damned blow over the face. His son, as rude as he was, would not strike his father, but strikes over the face the gentleman that sat next to him and said, "Box about: Twill come to my father anon."

—JOHN AUBREY

✦✦✦

I didn't make Dale Jr. go be a racer. The kid wanted to be a racer. I'd just as soon him be a doctor, a preacher, or whatever. I'm not sure I'd want him to be a lawyer.

—DALE EARNHARDT

✦✦

Before I was married, I had a hundred theories about raising children and no children. Now, I have three children and no theories.

—JOHN WILMOT

✦✦✦

A father is a man who carries pictures where his money used to be.
—ANONYMOUS

++

The place of the father in the modern suburban family is a very small one, particularly if he plays golf.
—BERTRAND RUSSELL

+++

A father is always making his baby into a little woman.
And when she is a woman, he turns her back again.
—ENID BAGNOLD

++

My father never raised his hand to any one of his children, except in self-defense.
—FRED ALLEN

+++

When I was a kid, I used to imagine animals running under my bed.
I told my dad, and he solved the problem quickly. He cut the legs off the bed.
—LOU BROCK

++

My father carries around the picture of the kid that came with the wallet.
—RODNEY DANGERFIELD

+++

Undeservedly you will atone for the sins of your fathers.
—HORACE

✦✦

I grew up to have my father's looks, my father's speech patterns, my
father's posture, my father's walk, my father's opinions,
and my mother's contempt for my father.
—JULES FEIFFER

✦✦✦

My father hated radio and he could not wait for television to be
invented so that he could hate that, too.
—PETER DE VRIES

✦✦

My father confused me. From the ages of one to seven, I thought my
name was Jesus Christ!
—BILL COSBY

✦✦✦

My father only hit me once—but he used a Volvo.
—BOB MONKHOUSE

✦✦

Dad always thought laughter was the best medicine, which I guess is
why several of us died of tuberculosis.
—JACK HANDY

✦✦✦

I've got two wonderful children—two out of five isn't bad, right?
—HENNY YOUNGMAN

✦✦

I never got along with my dad. Kids used to come up to me and say, "My dad can beat up your dad." I'd say, "Yeah? When?"
—BILL HICKS

+++

It's not easy to juggle a pregnant wife and a troubled child, but somehow I managed to fit in eight hours of TV a day.
—HOMER SIMPSON, *THE SIMPSONS*

++

I remember the time I was kidnapped and they sent a piece of my finger to my father. He said he wanted more proof.
—RODNEY DANGERFIELD

+++

Perhaps host and guest is really the happiest relation for a father and son.
—EVELYN WAUGH

++

I have seen more men destroyed by the desire to have a wife and child and to keep them in comfort than I have seen destroyed by drinks and harlots.
—WILLIAM BUTLER YEATS

+++

Fathers should never be seen nor heard. That is the only proper basis for family life.
—OSCAR WILDE

++

Top 10 Things Fathers Are Responsible for:

1. Sports
2. Teaching kids how to defend themselves
3. Movies
4. Beer (to relax from all the work it took for 1–3)
5. See Mom's list
6. See Mom's list
7. See Mom's list
8. See Mom's list
9. See Mom's list
10. See Mom's list

I can't get past the fact that food is now coming out of my wife's breasts. What was once essentially an entertainment center is now a juice bar.
—PAUL KRUGMAN

+++

My father would say things that made no sense, like, "If I were the last person on earth, some moron would turn left in front of me!"
—LOUIE ANDERSON

++

My wife just let me know I'm about to become a father for the first time. The bad news is we already have two kids.
—BRIAN KILEY

+++

My father was cheap. He'd make us Hamburger Helper with no hamburger.
—A. J. JAMAL

++

My dad said he had a tough childhood. He had to walk twenty miles to school in five feet of snow . . . and he was only four feet tall.
—DANA EAGLE

+++

When you're young, you think your dad is Superman. When you grow up, you realize he's just a guy who wears a cape.
DAVE ATTELL

++

My father didn't ask me to leave home. He took me down to the highway and pointed.
—HENNY YOUNGMAN

+++

My dad's pants kept creeping up on him. By the time he was sixty-five, he was just a pair of pants and a head.
—JEFF ALTMAN

++

I have mixed emotions when I receive my Father's Day gifts. I'm glad my children remember me; I'm disappointed that they actually think I dress that way.
—MIKE DUGAN

+++

Father's Day: For that lethal combination of alcohol and
new power tools.
—DAVID LETTERMAN

✦✦

I was raised just by my mother. My father died when I was eight years
old . . . at least, that's what he told us
in the letter.
—DREW CAREY

✦✦✦

I'm getting ready to be a parent. I just turned thirty and
I'm getting tired of mowing my grass.
—JEFF FOXWORTHY

✦✦

Sorry, Meg. Daddy loves ya, but Daddy also loves *Star Trek*, and in all
fairness, *Star Trek* was here first.
—PETER GRIFFIN, *FAMILY GUY*

✦✦✦

A father is a banker provided by nature.
—FRENCH PROVERB

✦✦

My father was frightened of his father, I was frightened of my father,
and I am damned well going to see to it that
my children are frightened of me.
—KING GEORGE V

✦✦✦

The child had every toy his father wanted.
—ROBERT C. WHITTEN

++

When I was born, my father spent three weeks trying to find a
loophole in my birth certificate.
—JACKIE VERNON

+++

He became a father today. There'll be hell to pay
if his wife finds out.
—ANONYMOUS

++

Today, while the titular head of the family may still be the father,
everyone knows that he is little more than chairman, at most, of the
entertainment committee.
—ASHLEY MONTAGU

+++

The fundamental defect of fathers is that they want their children to
be a credit to them.
—BERTRAND RUSSELL

++

It is a wise child that knows its own father, and an
unusual one that unreservedly approves of him.
—MARK TWAIN

+++

Watching your daughter being collected by her date feels like handing over a million dollar Stradivarius to a gorilla.
—JIM BISHOP

◆◆

I have adapted the philosophy of Genghis Khan, "Give a man a fish and he eats for a day, teach a man to fish and he eats forever." My slogan is, "Show a teenage boy a gun, and he'll have your daughter home by 11:30."
—SINBAD

◆◆◆

I married your mother because I wanted children.
Imagine my disappointment when you arrived.
—GROUCHO MARX

◆◆

A father is a man who expects his son to be as good a man as he meant to be.
—FRANK A. CLARK

◆◆◆

Match the Quote to the Movie: Father Edition[54]

A. *Fight Club*   D. *3 Men and a Baby*

B. *Father of the Bride*   E. *A Chorus Line*

C. *Empire Falls*

~+~

1. -Drive carefully. And don't forget to fasten your condom.
   -Dad!
   -Seat belt! I meant—I meant seat belt.
2. I couldn't catch a ball if it had Elmer's Glue all over it. And my father had to be this ex-football star. He didn't know what to tell his friends, so he told them all I had polio. On Father's Day, I used to limp for him.
3. All we have to do is feed it, it'll shut up.
4. Shut up! Our fathers were our models for God. If our fathers bailed, what does that tell you about God?
5. To tell you the truth, I would rather have a complete idiot for a child than an ingrate.

THE BOOK OF
SEX

Marriage

Getting married for sex is like buying a 747
for the free peanuts.
—JEFF FOXWORTHY

✦✦✦

A husband is what is left of a lover after the
nerve has been extracted.
—HELEN ROWLAND

✦✦

Bachelors know more about women than
married men; if they didn't, they'd be married too.
—H. L. MENCKEN

✦✦✦

A man in love is incomplete until he is married.
Then he is finished.
—ZSA ZSA GABOR

✦✦

Honeymoon: A short period of doting between
dating and debting.
—MIKE BINDER

✦✦✦

These days, the honeymoon is rehearsed
much more often than the wedding.
—P. J. O'ROURKE

~*~

*A honeymoon couple goes to a hotel and asks for a suite.
"Bridal?" asks the desk clerk. "No thanks," replies the
bride, "I'll just hang on to his shoulders."*

~*~

Sex drive: A physical craving that begins
in adolescence and ends in marriage.
—ROBERT BYRNE

**

I blame my mother for my poor sex life. All she told me was "the man
goes on top and the woman underneath." For years, my husband and I
slept in bunk beds.
—JOAN RIVERS

***

Never get married in the morning, because
you never know who you'll meet that night.
—PAUL HORNUNG

**

I never knew what real happiness was until
I got married. By then it was too late.
—MAX KAUFFMAN

***

The term "sex addict" makes it sound like
sex is a drug. And after twenty-three years of marriage,
in my house it's a controlled substance.
—BOBBY SLAYTON

**

Before I married my husband, I'd never fallen in love, although I'd
stepped in it a few times.

—RITA RUDNER

✦✦✦

I came from a big family. As a matter of fact, I never got to sleep
alone until I was married.

—LEWIS GRIZZARD

✦✦

~✦~

*After twenty years of marriage, a couple was lying in
bed one evening, when the woman felt her husband
begin to fondle her in ways he hadn't in quite some time.
It almost tickled as his fingers started at her neck and
then began moving down past the small of her back. He
then caressed her shoulders and neck, slowly worked his
hand down over her breasts, stopping just over her lower
stomach. He then proceeded to place his hand on her
left inner arm, caressed past the side of her breast again,
working down her side, past gently over her buttock, and
down her leg to her calf. Then, he proceeded up her inner
thigh, stopping just at the uppermost portion of her leg.
He continued in the same manner on her right side and
then suddenly stopped, rolled over, and became silent.
As she had become quite aroused by this caressing, she
asked in a loving voice, "Honey, that was wonderful.
Why did you stop?"*

"I found the remote."

~✦~

Sexual Indiscretions Match Box[57]

A. John Edwards	D. Larry Craig
B. Amy Fisher	E. David Letterman
C. Marv Albert	F. Elizabeth Taylor

~◆~

1. A sportscaster who became the butt of jokes when he was accused of sodomy and other bizarre sexual proclivities by a woman with whom he had a decade-long affair. His longtime girlfriend stood by him, and they recently married. That's what I call true love.

2. This movie star was married eight times to seven husbands. When her third husband died, she married his best friend (who was already married to someone else). They divorced; she married another film star whom she divorced, remarried, and divorced again. Two more to go.[58]

3. A married senator, with a strong anti-gay platform, allegedly caught in an airport men's room using his foot to tap out sexual preferences to the FBI agent in the next stall. He says he was just picking up a piece of paper.[59]

4. A complete unknown, she entered into a love tryst at seventeen with a thirty-six-year-old married mechanic and then shot and seriously injured his wife. Also had a sex tape. Still unknown.

5. A strong family-values presidential candidate, he was the subject of a sex tape with his mistress, who was pregnant with his love child at

---

57   1. C, 2. F, 3. D, 4. B, 5. A, 6. E
58   When you can't sleep, count her husbands.
59   Yeah, a mash note.

the time. Meanwhile, his wife was dying of cancer. Whaddaya think of those values?

6. After being outed by a news staffer, this married television host and comedian confessed to finding his fun at the office through affairs with several members of his staff.

Husbands think we should know where everything is—
like the uterus is a tracking device. He asks me, "Do we
have any Cheerios left?" Like he can't go over to the
sofa cushion and lift it himself.
—ROSEANNE BARR

+++

How to Seduce Your Wife:

Compliment her, cuddle her, kiss her, caress her, stroke her, tease her, comfort her, protect her, hug her, hold her, wine and dine her, buy things for her, listen to her, care for her, stand by her, support her, buy flowers for her, go to the ends of the earth for her . . .

How to Seduce Your Husband:

Show up naked. Bring beer.

Marriage is like a bank account.
You put it in, you take it out, you lose interest.
—IRWIN COREY

++

Marriage is an alliance entered into by a man
who can't sleep with the window shut, and a woman
who can't sleep with the window open.
—GEORGE BERNARD SHAW

+++

Marriage marks the end of many short follies—
being one long stupidity.
—FRIEDRICH NIETZSCHE[60]

++

As I grow older and older
And totter towards the tomb,
I find that I care less and less
Who goes to bed with whom.
—DOROTHY L. SAYERS

+++

It destroys one's nerves to be amiable every
day to the same human being.
—BENJAMIN DISRAELI

++

If you made a list of the reasons why any couple
got married, and another list of the reasons for
their divorce, you'd have a hell of a lot of overlapping.
—MIGNON MCLAUGHLIN

+++

---

[60]   What happened to "what doesn't kill me makes me stronger"?

All marriages are happy. It's the living together afterward that causes all the trouble.
—RAYMOND HULL

♦♦

Marriage ceremony: an incredible metaphysical sham of watching God and the law being dragged into the affairs of your family.
—O. C. OGILVIE

~♦~

Robert Schimmel's wife told him about a hot book about finding a woman's G-spot. "I went to a bookstore. I couldn't even find the book."

~♦~

That quiet mutual gaze of a trusting husband and
wife is like the first moment of rest or refuge
from a great weariness or a great danger.
—GEORGE ELIOT

♦♦♦

I hear love is entirely a matter of chemistry . . . must be why my wife treats me like toxic waste.
—DAVID BISONETTE

~♦~

Wife: Why don't you ever call out my name when we're making love?
Husband: Because I don't want to wake you.

~♦~

Love: A temporary insanity curable by marriage.
—AMBROSE BIERCE, *THE DEVIL'S DICTIONARY*

♦♦

Married life teaches one invaluable lesson: to think
of things far enough ahead not to say them.
—JEFFERSON MACHAMER

✦✦✦

Early on, he let her know who was the boss. He looked her right in
the eye and clearly said, "You're the boss."
—ANONYMOUS

✦✦

In Pursuit of Sex, Men Will . . .

➢ GO SHOE SHOPPING—"No, they're very different than
the seven other pairs in brown you looked at. I completely
get the nuance of ecru."

➢ CLEAN THE BATHROOM—"I love the smell of Pine-
Sol in the morning . . . smells like . . . cleanliness. And I will
definitely put all three hundred of your products back where
they were."

➢ WATCH THE NEIGHBOR'S KIDS—"Cool! Now
I finally have a reason to watch six hours of *SpongeBob
SquarePants* and *Veggie Tales*."

➢ EAT HEALTHY—"Yes, please bring me another helping
of that spinach-kale-broccoli-asparagus salad shit, er . . . I
mean, wow, tastes amazing!"

➢ THROW AWAY PICTURES OF OLD GIRL-
FRIENDS—"No, babe, I threw those away. That box way
up on that shelf in the garage that you can't reach is all the
birthday cards you've sent me."

- ➤ WATCH A CHICK FLICK—"No, I really do think that Julia Roberts or Sandra Bullock or Natalie Portman *is* the modern-day Clint Eastwood. Love to go."

- ➤ HAVE DINNER AT HER MOTHER'S—"Of course, it's been too long since I examined every fault I have. I can play poker with the guys anytime."

- ➤ NOT LAUGH AT TASTELESS JOKES—"Not funny. After all, blondes have feelings too. I'm appalled."

- ➤ GO GROCERY SHOPPING—"Sure, I'll get your tampons and Midol. If I can't find the size box you need, I can always ask the clerk."

- ➤ DRESS UP TO GO OUT, EVEN THOUGH IT'S NOT A WEDDING OR A FUNERAL—"Yeah, this suit makes me feel great, babe. It's just like being back at work."

- ➤ WATCH JIMMY FALLON INSTEAD OF LETTER-MAN—"I can totally see it now: he *is* cuter."

- ➤ ADMIT A MISTAKE—(Hey, let's not get carried away. After all, it's only sex ... only sex ... only ...) "Totally my fault, hon. Won't happen again."

I bought my wife a sex manual but half the pages
were missing. We went straight from foreplay
to postnatal depression.
—BOB MONKHOUSE

✦✦✦

So heavy is the chain of wedlock that it needs
two to carry it, and sometimes three.
—ALEXANDRE DUMAS[61]

++

The total amount of undesired sex endured by women is probably
greater in marriage than in prostitution.
—BERTRAND RUSSELL

+++

Women like silent men; they think they're listening.
—GEORGE CARLIN

~+~

*A husband was feeling horny one evening, but his wife
pushed him away. "Sorry, honey, but I have a gynecolo-
gist's appointment in the morning, and I want to stay
fresh." He nuzzled up to her again. "You don't have a
dental appointment, do you?"*

~+~

I'd marry again if I found a man who had fifteen million dollars and
would sign over half of it to me before the marriage . . . and guarantee
he'd be dead within the year.
—BETTE DAVIS

++

Marriage isn't all that it's cracked up to be. Let me tell you, honestly.
Marriage is probably the chief cause of divorce.
—FRANK BURNS, *M·A·S·H*

+++

---

61 Whole new perspective on *The Three Musketeers*; no?

Snarkin' the News:

↔ A California scientist has invented a lipstick that turns bright crimson on the lips of the woman wearing it when she's in the mood for sex. But be careful. He gave one to his girlfriend, and when he came home, his wife wanted to know why all the blood was rushing to his head.

↔ A man went skinny-dipping on a beach in New Zealand. Afterward, he fell asleep on the beach. He was awakened by a poisonous spider biting his penis. It swelled to six times its normal size. Now he has the twelve inches his wife has always wanted.

↔ Two women teachers in South Carolina were arrested recently for having sex and drug parties with their students over the summer. Guess they were tired of reading boring "What I Did on My Summer Vacation" essays and wanted to spice things up.

If variety is the spice of life, marriage is a big can
of leftover Spam.
—JOHNNY CARSON

++

After ten years of marriage, being good in bed means you don't steal
the covers.
—BRENDA DAVIDSON

+++

Housework is like bad sex. Every time I do it, I swear I will never do it again. Until the next time company comes.

—MARILYN SOKOL

♦♦

The trouble with some women is that they get all excited about nothing—and then marry him.

—CHER

~♦~

A father walks into his son's room and finds the boy pleasuring himself. He says, "Son, if you don't stop, you'll go blind!" "Dad, I'm over here!"

~♦~

The reason for much matrimony is patrimony.

—OGDEN NASH

♦♦♦

Things Not to Say During Sex

➤ You woke me up for that?

➤ Do you smell something burning?

➤ Try breathing through your nose.

➤ Can you please pass me the remote control?

➤ On second thought, let's turn off the lights.

➤ And to think—I was trying to pick up your friend!

I got married, and we had a baby nine months and ten seconds later.
—JAYNE MANSFIELD

✦✦

While redecorating, I realized my wife and I have dramatically different tastes in furniture. She wanted to keep the pieces that reflected the French provincial theme she was creating; I wanted to keep the stuff we'd had sex on.
—BRAD OSBERG

~✦~

A little boy gets up to go to the bathroom in the middle of the night. As he passes his parents' bedroom, he peeks in through the keyhole. He watches for a moment and then continues on down the hallway, saying to himself, "Boy, and she gets mad at me for sucking my thumb."

~✦~

Kids. They're not easy. But there has to be some penalty for sex.
—BILL MAHER

~✦~

A mother took her young daughter to the zoo. When they reached the elephant enclosure, the bull elephant looked angry and, to the embarrassment of the mother, had a huge erection. "Do you think he'll charge?" asked the little girl. "Well, I think he'd be entitled to," sighed her mother.

~✦~

Don't bother discussing sex with small children.
They rarely have anything to add.
—FRAN LEBOWITZ

✦✦✦

I believe in making the world safe for our children
but not our children's children, because I don't
think children should be having sex.
—JACK HANDEY

✦✦

There's only one way to have a happy marriage and as soon as I learn
what it is I'll get married again.
—CLINT EASTWOOD

✦✦✦

~✦~

*A couple has just had sex. The woman says, "If I got
pregnant, what would we call the baby?" The man takes
off his condom, ties it in a knot, and flushes it down
the toilet. "Well, if he can get out of that, we'll call him
Houdini."*

~✦~

Do you know what it means to come home to a little affection, a little
tenderness, and a little sympathy?
It means you're in the wrong house.
—JEFF FOXWORTHY

✦✦

The conception of two people living together for twenty-five years
without having a cross word suggests a lack of spirit only to be
admired in sheep.
—ALAN PATRICK HERBERT

✦✦✦

I wonder, among all the tangles of this mortal coil, which one contains
tighter knots to undo, and consequently suggests more tugging, and
pain, and diversified elements of misery, than the marriage tie.
—EDITH WHARTON

✦✦

One man's folly is another man's wife.
—HELEN ROWLAND

✦✦✦

We were happily married for eight months. Unfortunately, we were
married for four and a half years.
—NICK FALDO

✦✦

In Hollywood a marriage is a success if it outlasts milk.
—RITA RUDNER

~✦~

*A man walks into the bedroom with a sheep under his
arm. His wife is lying in bed, reading. "This is the pig
I have sex with when you've got a headache," the man
says. "I think you'll find that's a sheep," the wife says.
"Yes, and I was talking to it, not you."*

~✦~

I know nothing about sex because I was always married.
—ZSA ZSA GABOR

✦✦✦

Remember, that if thou marry for beauty, thou bindest thyself all thy life for that which perchance will neither last nor please thee one year; and when thou hast it, it will be to thee of no price at all; for the desire dieth when it is attained, and the affection perisheth when it is satisfied.
—SIR WALTER RALEIGH[62]

✦✦

Such is the common process of marriage. A youth and maiden exchange meeting by chance, or brought together by artifice, exchange glances, reciprocate civilities, go home, and dream of one another. Having little to divert attention, or diversify thought, they find themselves uneasy when they are apart, and therefore conclude that they shall be happy together. They marry, and discover what nothing but voluntary blindness had before concealed; they wear out life in altercations, and charge nature with cruelty.
—SAMUEL JOHNSON

✦✦✦

American women expect to find in their husbands a perfection that English women only hope to find in their butlers.
—W. SOMERSET MAUGHAM

✦✦

---

[62] The man who gave us smokes after sex.

Snarkin' the Facts

> ➤ *Historical records show that even in 1850 BC, women attempted to practice birth control. The most common method was a mixture of crocodile dung and honey placed in the vagina in the hopes of preventing pregnancy. But the absolute best method of birth control was getting the man to collect the crocodile dung.*

> ➤ *The vibrator, a common sex toy for women, was originally designed in the nineteenth century as a medication to combat the anxiety-related symptoms of hysteria. There were batteries in the nineteenth century? Or did they just need to hire someone to shake them real fast?*

> ➤ *According to Alfred Kinsey's* Sexual Behavior in the Human Male, *81 percent of men say they have experienced nocturnal emissions. "Honey, I know I was calling my assistant's name, but it was you I was dreaming about, dressed as my assistant—I swear."*

> ➤ *Worldwide, sexually active adults report having sex an average of 103 times per year. That's twice a week. Given the law of averages, somebody's not ever getting out of bed.*

~❖~

Q. What is the difference between a bachelor and a married man?

A. Bachelor comes home, sees what's in the refrigerator, goes to bed. Married man comes home, sees what's in the bed, and goes to the refrigerator.

~❖~

Things NOT to Say at a Wedding

1. Hey, I think I saw that same dress at Costco!
2. What's the over/under on whether this one will take?
3. Gonna be some ugly kids, no?
4. Get a load of the brides/groom's mom . . . Thanksgiving's gonna be a hoot.
5. I hope they love the vibrator I gave them.
6. Who catered this, Taco Bell?
7. Hopefully there'll be his and her bathrooms and his won't have any mirrors.
8. It's a fairytale wedding—and her mom gets to be the ogre.
9. Is that a bump? Maybe we need to throw puffed rice.
10. His marriage vows will be silence and poverty.
11. It's not that he's going to live longer, it's just going to seem longer.
12. You know how many hookers he could have had for what this wedding costs?
13. What a fastidious couple. She's fast and he's hideous.

My wife and I were happy for twenty years. Then we met.
—RODNEY DANGERFIELD

✦✦✦

Music and Performing Arts

Men don't realize that if we're sleeping with them
on the first date, we're probably not interested
in seeing them again either.
—CHELSEA HANDLER

••

She got the gold mine, I got the shaft.
—JERRY REED

•••

Love is not the dying moan of a distant violin—it's the triumphant
twang of a bedspring.
—S. J. PERELMAN

••

I always knew Frank would end up in bed with a boy.
—AVA GARDNER ON SINATRA'S MARRIAGE
TO MIA FARROW

•••

Disco provides a rhythmic accompaniment for the activities of people who wish to gain access to each other for potential future reproduction.
—FRANK ZAPPA

++

Strippers should be role models for little girls. If only for the fact that they wax their assholes.
—SARAH SILVERMAN

+++

I'm not slutty at all. I've only slept with four men . . . and that was a weird night.
—AMY SCHUMER

++

You have between your legs the most
sensitive instrument known to man, and all
you can do is sit there and scratch it.
—SIR THOMAS BEECHAM TO A FEMALE CELLIST

+++

~+~

A man and a woman are lying in bed after a disappointing round of sex. "You've got a very small organ," says the woman. The man replies, "Yeah, well, I didn't know I'd be playing Carnegie Hall."

~+~

There's nothing better than good sex . . . but bad sex? A peanut-butter-and-jelly sandwich is better than bad sex.
—BILLY JOEL

++

Losing my virginity was a career move.
—MADONNA

+++

I'd like to meet the man who invented sex and
see what he's working on now.
—GEORGE CARLIN

++

Five Songs Guaranteed to Kill the Mood

1. "Who Let the Dogs Out," Baha Men
2. "Thong Song," Sisqó
3. "Don't Worry, Be Happy," Bobby McFerrin
4. "Smack My Bitch Up," Prodigy
5. "We Are the World," USA for Africa

The best things in life are free . . . try explaining
that to an angry hooker.
—DANIEL BOKOR

+++

Women say they want a man who knows
what a woman's worth. That's a pimp.
—RICH HALL

++

Don't leave a piece of jewelry at his house so you can go back and get it
later; he may be with his real girlfriend.
—AMY SEDARIS

+++

Oooh. Aaahhh. Get out.
—ANDREW DICE CLAY'S IMPRESSION OF
A ONE-NIGHT STAND

++

My girlfriend can count all the lovers she's had on one hand—
provided she's holding a calculator.
—TOM COTTER

+++

Oysters are supposed to enhance sexual performance, but they don't
work for me. Maybe I put them on too soon.
—GARRY SHANDLING

++

I'm saving the bass player for Omaha.
—JANIS JOPLIN

+++

You know more about a man in one night in
bed than in months of conversation.
—EDITH PIAF

++

I'm afraid of the video guy judging me because
I don't want him to think I'm some sort of a freaky
pervert. So now when I rent porn, I'll actually get
Dirty Debutantes and *Citizen Kane*. He knows
I'm a masturbating loser, but I'm a
sophisticated masturbating loser.
—MARC MARON

+++

Sexual Indiscretions Match Box[63]

A. Mackenzie Phillips	D. George Michael
B. Pamela Anderson	E. Kid Rock
C. Fred Durst	F. Rihanna

~+~

1. Limp Bizkit's front man sued when a repairman leaked his sex video. Not sure why—he could have proved once and for all that the name of his band wasn't based on his organ.
2. First, she was abused by her musician boyfriend, and then naked pictures appeared on the web. She defended them—and the boyfriend—by saying, "If you don't send your boyfriend naked pictures, then I feel bad for him." Ummm . . . okay.
3. Made not one but two sex tapes with rock stars of questionable talent if not endowment. Was then engaged to a third rock star. No report on his endowment.
4. Used both Oprah and a tell-all bio to reveal the news of a rape and subsequent decade-long affair with her pop star father.
5. A teen heartthrob that came out of the closet when he was caught and arrested for "lewd behavior" in the public toilet at a Beverly Hills park.
6. A tape of him getting a blow job on his tour bus never got to DVD, but maybe that's because it contained "no sex" according to his now-former pal, Scott Stapp of Creed (who was also involved in the "nonsexual" action, along with four female groupies).

---

[63] 1. C, 2. F, 3. B, 4. A, 5. D, 6. E

You know you gotta lose some weight when your
girlfriend wants to lick your titties.
—REGGIE MCFADDEN

++

Oral sex should be an Olympic sport because it's harder than curling,
and if you're good at it, you deserve a medal.
—LEWIS BLACK

+++

My girlfriend was complaining about my stamina in the sack, so I
popped six Viagra and drank a six-pack of Red Bull. Her funeral is
Tuesday.
—HARLAN WILLIAMS

++

Three minutes of serious sex and I need eight hours
of sleep and a giant bowl of Wheaties.
—RICHARD PRYOR

+++

I tried phone sex—it gave me an ear infection.
—RICHARD LEWIS

++

I told her the thing I loved most about her
was her mind . . . because that's what I told her
to get into bed with me.
—STEVEN WRIGHT

+++

I like my wine like my women—ready to pass out.
—ROBIN WILLIAMS

++

I think we can all agree that sleeping around
is a great way to meet people.
—CHELSEA HANDLER

+++

My boyfriend and I live together, which means we don't have sex—
ever. Now that the milk is free, we've both become lactose intolerant.
—MARGARET CHO

~+~

Q: What did the bowlegged doe say?
A: That's the last time I do that for ten bucks.

~+~

I want to get an abortion. But my boyfriend and
I are having trouble conceiving.
—SARAH SILVERMAN

++

Everybody loves you when they are about to come.
—MADONNA

+++

They're talking about banning cigarette smoking now in any place
that's used by ten or more people in a week, which, I guess, means that
Madonna can't even smoke in bed.
—BILL MAHER

++

True or False?

↔ A G-string is part of a violin.

↔ Coitus is a musical instrument.

↔ Kotex is a radio station in Texas.

What is love but a secondhand emotion?
—TINA TURNER

✦✦✦

Sex and drugs and rock and roll
Is all my brain and body need
Sex and drugs and rock and roll
Are very good indeed.
—IAN DURY

~✦~

Q: What is two hundred feet long and has no pubic hair?
A: The front row at a Jonas Brothers concert.

~✦~

His finest hour lasted a minute and a half.
—PHYLLIS DILLER

✦✦

I don't know if it's the weather or what's going on—the summer or something like that—but recently I've been feeling extremely bisexual. I don't know what it is. I don't know what's going on, but I walked down the street, and suddenly, the ladies are looking awfully good to me.

—ANDY KINDLER

~+~

Snarkin' the News

↔ Ah yes, Courtney Love . . . I mean Courtney Michelle . . . said in an interview that homely girls are better at sex, that "us girls who grew up that way try harder. Pretty girls just lay there." I'm sure she has firsthand information . . . more people have gone down on her than on the *Titanic*.

↔ Lady Gaga said in an interview in *Vanity Fair* that she's refraining from sex because she worried that "if I sleep with someone, they're going to take my creativity away through my vagina." Off by inches, sweetie.

↔ George Michael has been arrested again in London for "possession of cannabis and driving while unfit through drink or drugs." And guess what? It was in a bathroom! He should do a kids' book—*Everybody Poops . . . and Gets High*.

↔ Kevin Federline is expecting his fifth child—oops, I did it again . . . and again . . . and again . . .

Divorce

My husband and I had our best sex during our divorce. It was like cheating on our lawyers.
—PRICILLA LOPEZ

~•~

A lonely divorcee was driving home from work and saw a man hitchhiking. She picked him up, and they started talking.

"What do you do?" she asked him.

"I recently escaped from prison, where I was serving a life sentence for killing my wife."

"Oh, so you're available?"

~•~

Bigamy is having one husband or wife too many.

Monogamy is the same.
—OSCAR WILDE

•••

Alimony: The ransom that the happy pay to the devil.
—H. L. MENCKEN

••

Alimony is the screwing you get for the screwing you got.

+++

My divorce came to me as a complete surprise. That's what happens when you haven't been home in eighteen years.
—LEE TRAVINO

++

You mean, apart from my own?
—ZSA ZSA GABOR, WHEN ASKED HOW MANY HUSBANDS SHE'D HAD

+++

Things Not to Say During Sex

➤ You're almost as good as my ex!

➤ You look younger than you feel.

➤ Perhaps you're just out of practice.

➤ And to think, I didn't even have to buy you dinner!

➤ I have a confession . . .

➤ I'll tell you whom I'm fantasizing about if you tell me whom you're fantasizing about . . .

➤ Petroleum jelly or no petroleum jelly, I said no.

➤ Keep it down . . . my mother is a light sleeper . . .

➤ My old girlfriend used to do it a *lot* longer!

Nothing is better for the spirit or the body than a love affair. It elevates thoughts and flattens stomachs.
—BARBARA HOWAR

++

I enjoy dating married people because they never want anything kinky, like breakfast.
—JONI RODGERS

~+~

Q. How do you make your wife scream while having sex?

A. Call her and tell her.

~+~

Adultery is the most conventional way
to rise above the unconventional.
—VLADIMIR NABOKOV

+++

A man can have two, maybe three, affairs while
he's married. After that, you're cheating.
—YVES MONTAND

++

There are times not to flirt. When you're sick. When you're with
children. When you're on the witness stand.
—JOYCE JILLSON

+++

Thou shalt not commit adultery . . . unless in the mood.
—W. C. FIELDS

++

I ran into my ex today . . . put it in reverse
and did it again.

✦✦✦

I'm an excellent housekeeper. Every time
I get divorced, I keep the house.
—ZSA ZSA GABOR

✦✦

I know many married men, I even know a few happily married men,
but I don't know one who wouldn't fall
down the first open manhole running after the first pretty girl who
gives him a wink.
—GEORGE JEAN NATHAN

✦✦✦

A sure sign that a man is going to be unfaithful
is if he has a penis.
—JO BRAND

~✦~

A man and his young wife were in divorce court, but the custody of their children posed a problem. The mother gets up and says to the judge that since she brought the children into this world, she should retain custody of them. The man also wanted custody of his children, so the judge asked for his justification. After a long silence, the man slowly rose from his chair and replied, "Your Honor, when I put a dollar in a vending machine and a Coke comes out, does the Coke belong to me or the machine?"

~✦~

Snarkin' the Facts

➢ *Outside of the bedroom, the most common place for adults in the United States to have sex is the car. Hence the reason the stick shift will be a thing of the past.*

➢ *Statistics suggest that approximately one in every five Americans has indulged in sex with a colleague at work. Boy, that person gets around.*

➢ *Viagra, the well-known blue pill designed to help with erectile dysfunction, made $411 million in profits within the first three months of its release in 1998 before going on to make $1.8 billion in 2003. And it's just going to keep going up and up. And staying up.*

➢ *Having sex can make a woman look younger and more attractive. Leaving the lights off more than triples those odds.*

➢ *The typical person spends about six hundred hours having sex between the ages of twenty and seventy. (So if your husband or wife disappears for twenty-five days, you know what they're doing.)*

My wife stopped pretending to have orgasms years ago. That's all right with me, though, because it allowed me to stop pretending that I cared.

—MIKE RANSTON

✦✦✦

My wife used to love to talk to me during sex. The other day she called me from a motel.

—RODNEY DANGERFIELD

✦✦

I once knew a woman who offered her honor
So I honored her offer
And all night long I was on her and off her.

—ANONYMOUS

✦✦✦

I just broke up with someone, and the last thing she said to me was, "You'll never find anyone like me again!" I'm thinking, *I should hope not! If I don't want you, why would I want someone like you?*

—KEITH SWEAT

✦✦

Signs That Your Lover Is Bored:

➢ Passionless kisses

➢ Frequent sighing

➢ Moved, left no forwarding address

—MATT GROENING

Seven Kinds of Sex

> ➤ SMURF SEX—The first throes of passion, when you're fucking until you're blue in the face.

> ➤ KITCHEN SEX—You're definitely a couple, but you're still attracted enough to be overcome with desire while making dinner.

> ➤ BEDROOM SEX—Her thong has become a brief, he's wearing pajamas, and you usually have sex in bed.

> ➤ RELIGIOUS SEX—Nun in the morning, nun in the afternoon, and nun at night.

> ➤ HALLWAY SEX—You've been together too long. When you pass each other in the hallway, you say "fuck you."

> ➤ COURTROOM SEX—Your soon-to-be ex-wife and her lawyer screw you in the divorce court in front of many people and for every penny you've got.

> ➤ SOCIAL SECURITY SEX—Back in the game, you now get a little each month. But it's not enough to live on.

When people say, "You're breaking my heart," more often than not, they mean, "You're breaking my balls."

—JEFFREY BERNARD

~+~

Reason for divorce #1: You go to the Hallmark store and ask, "Can you show me to the 'controlling bitch' section?"

Reason for divorce #2: You find an invoice in your spouse's dresser drawer for a hitman.

~+~

I don't see any reason for marriage when there is divorce.

—CATHERINE DENEUVE

++

I hardly said a word to my wife until I said "yes" to divorce.

—JOHN MILIUS

+++

I swear, if you existed I'd divorce you.

—EDWARD ALBEE

++

Roseanne Barr

➤ You may marry the man of your dreams, but fourteen years later, you're married to a couch that burps.

➤ Men read maps better than women because men can understand the concept of an inch equaling a hundred miles.

➤ There are men who like to dress up as women, and when they do, they can no longer parallel park.

> The fastest way to a man's heart is through his chest.

> I'm only upset that I'm not a widow (on her divorce from Tom Arnold)

A bachelor never quite gets over the idea that he is a thing of beauty and a boy forever.
—HELEN ROWLAND

+++

Love makes the time pass. Time makes love pass.
—EURIPEDES

~+~

During a routine search, a stowaway girl was discovered by the captain. "What are you doing here?" the Captain asked. "I have an arrangement with one of the sailors," she explained. "I got to go to Europe because he's screwing me." "In more ways than one, lady," said the captain. "This is the Staten Island Ferry."

~+~

True or False?

> "Vagina" is a medical term used to describe heart trouble.

> "Anus" is the Latin word for "yearly."

> A diaphragm is a drawing in geometry.

> An enema is someone who is not your friend.

Love is the self-delusion we manufacture to justify the trouble we take
to have sex.
—DANIEL S. GREENBERG

♦♦

Why do Jewish divorces cost so much? They're worth it.
—HENNY YOUNGMAN

♦♦♦

I don't think I'll get married again. I'll just find a woman I don't like
and buy her a house.
—LEWIS GRIZZARD

♦♦

We would have broken up except for the children. Who were the
children? Well, she and I were.
—MORT SAHL

♦♦♦

~♦~

*Heinrich Heine left his entire estate to his wife on the
condition she marry again, because, according to Heine,
"There will be at least one man who will regret my death."*

~♦~

What scares me about divorce is my children might put me in a home
for unwed mothers.
—TERESSA SKELTON

♦♦

You don't know a woman till you've met her in court.
—NORMAN MAILER

+++

When two people are under the influence of the most violent, most
insane, most delusive, and most transient of passions, they are
required to swear that they will remain in that excited, abnormal, and
exhausting condition continuously until death do them part.
—GEORGE BERNARD SHAW

++

Love is a grave mental disease.
—PLATO

+++

THE BOOK OF
CHRISTMAS

Merriment
(MARKETING)

Christmas is the Disneyfication of Christianity.
—DON CUPITT

✦✦

Christmas is a race to see which gives out first—your money
or your feet.
—ANONYMOUS

✦✦✦

A Christmas shopper's complaint is
one of long-standing.
—JAY LENO

✦✦

For those of you out there who are thinking about the Hanukkah-
versus-Christmas thing, let me tell you this: Quite honestly—and
this comes from an experiment with a two-and-a-half-year-old—
Christmas *blows the doors* off of Hanukkah.
—JON STEWART

✦✦✦

Hanukkah Books You'll Never See

➢ **The Schmuck Who Stole Hanukkah:** The story of a moron that tries to enter the village of Schvantzville to steal all the toys but can't seem to pick the "big" night.

➢ **Good Night, Moon-orah:** A very *short* book, it follows a child on each night as she says good night to her presents. Chapter 1: "Good Night, Dreidel." End of chapter. Chapter 2: "Good Night, Chocolate Gelt in a Mesh Bag." End of chapter. And so on.

➢ **The Runaway Dreidel:** A dreidel wants to run away because everyone thinks he's just a cheap little top with writing on it.

➢ **The Giving Tree (But Just a Little):** A children's book that is instructional for parents, it tells the story of a little Jewish boy who befriends a tree and is institutionalized for it.

➢ **The Big Book of Mackabee Pop-ups:** Oy, too many swords. You'll put your eye out.

Oh look, yet another Christmas TV special! How touching to have the meaning of Christmas brought to us by cola, fast food, and beer . . . Who'd have ever guessed that product consumption, popular entertainment, and spirituality would mix so harmoniously?

—BILL WATTERSON

♦♦

Anyone who believes that men are the equal of women has never seen a man trying to wrap a Christmas present.

—ANONYMOUS

+++

There is nothing sadder in this world than to wake Christmas morning and not be a child.

—ERMA BOMBECK

++

The three wise men sound very generous, but what you've got to remember is that those gifts were joint Christmas and birthday presents.

—JIMMY CARR

+++

Really Bad Holiday Ideas

1. Christmas ads with smoking Santas
2. Xmas cards with naked pics of you and family
3. Gifting a mausoleum for Christmas (just $10,000!)
4. Musical holly/wreaths/poinsettias
5. Mistletoe belt

I was so poor growing up if I hadn't been born a boy, I would have had nothing to play with on Christmas Day.

—RODNEY DANGERFIELD

++

Nothing's as mean as giving a small child
something useful for Christmas.
—KIN HUBBARD

✦✦✦

Probably the worst thing about being Jewish during Christmastime
is shopping, because the lines are so long. They should have a Jewish
express line. "Look, I'm a Jew. It's not a gift. It's just paper towels!"
—SUE KOLINSKY

✦✦

The moment you stop believing in Santa Claus is the moment you
start getting clothes for Christmas.
—ANONYMOUS

✦✦✦

I'm giving everyone framed underwear for Christmas.
—ANDY WARHOL

✦✦

Christmas: A day set apart and consecrated to gluttony, drunkenness,
maudlin sentiment, gift-taking, public dullness, and domestic
behavior.
—AMBROSE BIERCE

✦✦✦

Tipping Notes

- ➤ Thanks so much for doing what you get paid for.

- ➤ Happy holidays. This is for another year of barely pass-able service.

- ➤ I appreciate the envelope with your name and address on it. Hard to reuse without a ton of Wite-Out, so here's a little somethin' . . .

- ➤ Happy Haveatcha and a merry guilt Trip.

- ➤ Here you are. Those ten hours of O. T. sure came in handy so I can do this for you.

There are a lot of things money can't buy. None of them are on my Christmas list.
—JOAN RIVERS

++

One Christmas, things were so bad in our house that I asked Santa for a yo-yo and all I got was a piece of string. My father told me it was a yo.
—BRENDAN O'CARROLL

+++

Who says shopping early avoids the rush? I did mine a full twelve months in advance, and the stores were just as busy as ever.
—GAVIN MCKERNAN

++

12 Days of Gifts

1. Islamic Poker[64]
2. Fairly Serious Putty
3. The Lil' Electrical Outlet Licker
4. 5200 Card Pickup: a card game that keeps the kids busy all day
5. Ginsu Boomerang
6. The Pee-wee Herman Pull Toy
7. Nintendo 63 (This one was pretty easy to come by this holiday, for some reason.)
8. Hasbro's Lil' Barber
9. Tickle Me Carrot Top
10. Angry Birds-Baked-in-a-Pie
11. Doggie Dentist kit
12. The screenplay to the last *Star Trek* movie—"Live Long Then Expire"

---

[64] Lose a hand? Lose a hand!

It makes one's mouth hurt to speak with
such forced merriment.
—DAVID SEDARIS

My father gave me a bat for Christmas. The first time I played with it,
it flew away.
—RODNEY DANGERFIELD

Phoebe: *You know, Chandler, you being here is the best
gift I could ask for Christmas.*
Chandler: *Aw, thanks, Pheebs.*
Phoebe: *Okay, now where's my real present?*
—FRIENDS

Oh, joy . . . Christmas Eve. By this time
tomorrow, millions of people, knee-deep in
tinsel and wrapping paper, will utter those
heartfelt words, "Is this all I got?"
—FRASIER

Christmas crept into Pine Cove like a creeping Christmas thing:
dragging garland, ribbon, and sleigh bells, oozing eggnog, reeking
of pine, and threatening festive doom like a cold sore under the
mistletoe.
—CHRISTOPHER MOORE

~♦~

For more than twenty-five years, Santa to the Stars Brady White earned thousands of dollars a night each December by playing Santa and taking Christmas requests from the rich and famous. White's most memorable moment? Madonna sat on his lap one year and asked to have her virginity back.[65]

~♦~

A lot of Americans got hi-definition televisions for Christmas, which means a lot more celebrities will be seeing their plastic surgeons this year.

—JOAN RIVERS

♦♦

~♦~

Santa asked the little girl what she wanted for Christmas.
"I want a Barbie and a G.I. Joe," said the girl.
"I thought Barbie comes with Ken?" asked Santa.
"No," she replied, "Barbie comes with G.I. Joe. She fakes it with Ken."

~♦~

---

[65] Not even Santa can make that happen.

Christmas Facts

➤ A Christmas club, a savings account in which a person deposits a fixed amount of money regularly to be used at Christmas for shopping, came about around 1905. It is now a source of much amusement for bank employees when you get your passbook and realize you could have made more interest with a lemonade stand.

➤ According to a 1995 survey, seven out of ten British dogs get Christmas gifts from their doting owners. That same survey revealed that only five of those ten dogs actually return those gifts for something else.

➤ Although many believe the Friday after Thanksgiving is the busiest shopping day of the year, it is not. It is the fifth to tenth busiest day. It is, however, the day when the murder rate goes up significantly in almost forty states.

I bought my brother some gift-wrap for Christmas. I took it to the gift wrap department and told them to wrap it, but in a different print so he would know when to stop unwrapping.

—STEVEN WRIGHT

✦✦✦

Snarkin' the Holidays

↪ "Merry Christmas"—not "Happy holidays" or "Season's greetings"—is once again OK to use.

↪ "Family trees"? Or worse, "holiday trees"? Not on my watch.

↪ What about Christmas songs? "Have Yourself a Merry Little Day of Winter"? "Frosty the Snowperson"? Or "Deck the Halls with Boughs of Unendangered Foliage"?

↪ You couldn't give a "bum" a handout for "the holidays" anymore . . . no, no, he's a *displaced person*.

↪ "Gee, Daddy, Santa Claus is really fat!" . . . "No, sweetie, he's got an *enlarged physical condition caused by a completely natural genetically induced hormonal imbalance*."

↪ "Look, Mom, an elf!" . . . "Now, now, that man is just *vertically challenged*."

↪ Tip the janitor? No, no, no . . . he's a *custodial artist*. Double whatever you were gonna give him.

Go ahead, say what you want, because it's beginning to feel a lot like that short period of time in December.

—THE AUTHOR

~♦~

Stan: Yeah, and you know, I think I learned something today. It doesn't matter if you're Christian or Jewish or atheist or Hindu. Christmas, still, is about one very important thing—

Cartman: Yeah, ham.

Stan: Christmas is about something much more important.

Kyle: What?

Stan: Presents.

Kyle: Hey man, if you're Jewish, you get presents for eight days!

Stan: Wow, really? Count me in!

Cartman: Yeah, I'll be a Jew too!

—SOUTH PARK

~♦~

Traditions
(SPIRIT)

~✦~

Frasier: Dad, what are you doing with that wreath?
Martin: I'm gonna hang it on the door like I always do.
Frasier: But it's plastic!
Martin: Of course it's plastic! Do you think a real one
would have lasted since 1967?
—FRASIER

~✦~

Last Christmas, I put up stockings.
All I got were Odor Eaters.
—RODNEY DANGERFIELD

✦✦

In the immortal words of Tiny Tim,
"God help us everyone!"
—GROUCHO MARX

✦✦✦

Most Texans think Hanukkah is some
sort of duck call.
—RICHARD LEWIS

++

I got a sweater for Christmas . . . I wanted a screamer or a moaner.
—ANONYMOUS

+++

Kiss her under the mistletoe? I wouldn't
kiss her under anesthetic.
—ANONYMOUS

++

I've learned that you can tell a lot about a person by the way (s)he
handles these three things: a rainy day, lost luggage, and tangled
Christmas tree lights.
—MAYA ANGELOU

+++

If "ifs" and "buts" were candy and nuts, wouldn't it be a merry
Christmas?
—DON MEREDITH

++

Well, what shall we hang, the holly
or each other?
—HENRY II, *THE LION IN WINTER*

+++

Brain Scan: Inside the Head of a Snowman

> ➤ I'm dreaming of a white Christmas . . .
>   I'm dreaming of a white Christmas . . .
>   I'm dreaming of a white Christmas . . .
>
> ➤ I'm dreaming of a white Christmas . . .
>   I'm dreaming of a white Christmas . . .
>   I'm dreaming of a white Christmas . . .
>
> ➤ I'm dreaming of a white Christmas . . .
>   I'm dreaming of a white Christmas . . .
>   I'm dreaming of a white Christmas . . .

Christmas Is . . .

A time for saying that Christmas is a time for doing things that one should, frankly, be doing anyway. "Christmas is a time for considering people less fortunate than ourselves." Oh, July and August aren't, is that it?
—STEPHEN FRY

++

A time when people of all religions come together to worship Jesus Christ.
—BART SIMPSON, *THE SIMPSONS*

+++

Hell in a stupid sweater.
—CARINA CHOCANO

++

Santa Claus and elves and stockings hung by the fireplace and good cheer and a big dinner and sugar cookies and gifts, gifts, and more gifts.
—BINNIE KIRSHENBAUM

+++

The collectivization of gaiety and the compulsory infliction of joy.
—CHRISTOPHER HITCHENS

++

The magical time of year when all your money disappears.
—HAL ROACH

+++

Awesome. First of all, you get to spend time with the ones you love. Secondly, you can get drunk and no one can say anything. Third, you give presents. What's better than giving presents? And fourth, getting presents. So four things. Not bad for one day. It's really the greatest day of all.
—MICHAEL SCOTT, *THE OFFICE*

++

People being helped by people other than me.
—JERRY SEINFELD

+++

Tradition. That's what you associate with Christmas: tradition. And drunk driving. And despair and lonliness. But mainly tradition.
—CHARLIE BROOKER

++

"The Little Drummer Boy" was playing in the background for what seemed like the third time in a row. I fought off an urge to beat that Little Drummer Boy senseless with his own drumsticks.
—DANA REINHARDT

+++

George Bernard Shaw

↔ I am sorry to have to introduce the subject of Christmas. It's an indecent subject; a cruel, gluttonous subject; a drunken, disorderly subject; a wasteful, disastrous subject; a wicked, cadging, lying, filthy, blasphemous, and demoralizing subject. Christmas is forced on a reluctant and disgusted nation by the shopkeepers and the press: on its own merits it would wither and shrivel in the fiery breath of universal hatred; and anyone who looked back to it would be turned into a pillar of greasy sausages.

↔ It is really an atrocious institution. We must be gluttonous because it is Christmas. We must be drunken because it is Christmas . . . We must buy things that nobody wants and give them to people we don't like; because the mass of the population, including the all-powerful middle-class tradesman, depends on a week of license and brigandage, waste and intemperance, to clear off its outstanding liabilities at the end of the year . . . As for me, I shall fly from it all tomorrow.

↔ Like all intelligent people, I greatly dislike Christmas. It revolts me to see a whole nation refrain from music for weeks together in order that every man may rifle his neighbour's pockets under cover of a ghastly pretence of festivity.

↔ A perpetual holiday is a good working definition of hell.

~•~

A Northern man was traveling through a small southern town when he found a "Nativity scene" that was created with great skill and talent. The only strange thing was that the three wise men were wearing firemen's helmets.

Totally unable to come up with a reason or explanation, he stopped at a 7-Eleven at the edge of town and asked the lady behind the counter about the helmets.

She exploded into a rage, yelling, "You darn Yankees never read your Bibles!"

The man said he had read the Bible many times but couldn't recall any mention of firemen.

She jerked her Bible from behind the counter, riffled through some pages, and finally jabbed her finger at a passage. "See, it says right here, 'The three wise man came from afar.'"

~•~

The Italian version? One Mary, one
Jesus, thirty-three wise guys.
—ANONYMOUS

++

Jeez, why are we talking about God and religion? It's Christmas!
—JACKIE, *ROSEANNE*

+++

~+~

A woman goes to the post office to buy stamps for her Chanukah cards. She says to the clerk, "May I have fifty Chanukah stamps?" The clerk says, "What denomination?" The woman says, "Oh my god. Has it come to this? Give me six Orthodox, twelve Conservative, and thirty-two Reform."

~+~

Being prepared is the secret of a harmonious Christmas. If Joseph had booked ahead, Jesus would not have been born in a stable.
—JILLY COOPER

++

~+~

Lucy: Merry Christmas, Charlie Brown. At this time of the year, I think we should put aside our differences and try to be kind.
Charlie Brown: Why does it have to be just this time of year? Can't it be all year round?

Lucy: What are you? Some kind of fanatic or something?

—PEANUTS

~♦~

It is my heart-warmed and world-embracing Christmas hope and
aspiration that all of us, the high, the low, the rich, the poor, the
admired, the despised, the loved, the hated, the civilized, the savage,
may eventually be gathered together in a heaven of everlasting rest
and peace and bliss, except the inventor of the telephone.

—MARK TWAIN

♦♦♦

~♦~

*During the first day of Hanukkah, two elderly Jewish
men were sitting in a wonderful deli frequented almost
exclusively by Jews in New York City. They were talking
among themselves in Yiddish—the colorful language of
Jews who came over from Eastern Europe.*

*A Chinese waiter, in New York for only a year, came
up and in fluent, impeccable Yiddish asked them if everything was okay and if they were enjoying the holiday.*

*The Jewish men were dumbfounded. "Where did
he ever learn such perfect Yiddish?" they both thought.
After they paid the bill, they asked the restaurant
manager, an old friend of theirs, "Where did our waiter
learn such fabulous Yiddish?"*

The manager looked around and leaned in so no one else would hear and said, "Shhhh. He thinks we're teaching him English."

~+~

~+~

Three men die in a car accident Christmas Eve. They all find themselves at the pearly gates waiting to enter heaven. On entering they must present something "Christmassy."

The first man searches his pocket and finds some mistletoe, so he is allowed in.

The second man presents some holly, so he is also allowed in.

The third man pulls out a pair of panties.

Confused at this last gesture, St. Peter asks, "How do these represent Christmas?"

The third man answered "They're Carol's."

~+~

Snarkin' the Holidays

Finally, out of the mall. Takes an hour, but it's good to be out and on the highway—which, frankly, isn't a whole lot better than the parking lot, but I see freedom. My heart rate slows, and my breathing becomes more regular. We've made it. We're free. That's when I hear those dreaded words: "Remember, the Yablonskis asked us to stop by for a drink."

I want to stop by and have a drink with *them* like I want to cough up a lung.

The after-shopping just-drop-by drink is like dancing in a body cast. I mean, it's dancing. It should be fun, but it just doesn't quite make it. And the Yablonskis and their ilk are people who usually brag about having all their shopping finished. Their house is decorated with thousands of stuffed rats in Christmas garb. (What the hell is that about?) Their tree is perfect. They have a perfect roaring fire and warm brandy liquor laced with . . . I don't know, honey or lemon. (Because you can't find a better way to screw up liquor?)

I hate this. I am in hell.

—THE AUTHOR

Christmas Facts

➤ "Hot cockles" was a popular game at Christmas in medieval times. It was a game in which the other players took turns striking the blindfolded player, who had to guess the name of the person delivering each blow. Hot cockles was still a Christmas pastime until the Victorian era and has only recently been reintroduced as a method of preparation for holiday shopping.

➤ According to the National Christmas Tree Association, Americans buy 37.1 million real Christmas trees each year. On January 2, the National Waste Management Association claims it picks up almost 36.9 million of said trees.

➤ After *A Christmas Carol*, Charles Dickens wrote several other Christmas stories, one each year, but none were as successful as the original. Among the least successful were *A Christmas Mildred*, *A Christmas Agnes*, and *A Christmas Bob*. Additionally, before settling on the name Tiny Tim, Dickens considered three other alliterative names: Little Larry, Puny Pete, Small Sam, Miniscule Marty, Wee Willie, and Malnourished Mark. Never had a chance.

➤ An average household in America will mail out twenty-eight Christmas cards each year and see twenty-eight cards return in their place. Because if you get twenty-seven back this year, you're mailing out twenty-seven cards next year.

December 25 is National Jews Go to the Movies Day.
—JON STEWART

++

President Obama held a ceremony at the White House to celebrate
the first night of Hanukkah. In response, Republicans said, "It's even
worse than we thought. He's a Jewish Muslim."
—CONAN O'BRIEN

+++

Did you ever notice that life seems to follow certain patterns? Like I
noticed that every year around this time, I hear Christmas music.
—TOM SIMS

++

I'm so riddled with the holiday spirit that the mere mention of
stocking filler sexually arouses me.
—JOHN WATERS

+++

Celebrities love the season of goodwill to all men. No need to put up
Christmas lights—they just crank up the power on the electric fence
until it's white hot.
—DAVID LETTERMAN

++

When decorating the tree, always use strings of cheap lights
manufactured in Third World nations that only recently found out
about electricity and have no words in their language for "fire code."
—DAVE BARRY

+++

Let's Go A-Caroling

- ➤ ALL I WANT FOR CHRISTMAS IS MY TWO FRONT TEETH. (On Amy Winehouse's Christmas list)

- ➤ ANGELS WE HAVE HEARD ON HIGH. (High on what? Angel dust? Nyuk, nyuk.)

- ➤ CHESTNUTS ROASTING ON AN OPEN FIRE. (Don't sit so close to the fire, you moron.)

- ➤ DO YOU HEAR WHAT I HEAR? (Really? I mean, really? You'd think you'd know better. Tell the world, go ahead. Damn gossip.)

- ➤ FROSTY THE SNOWMAN (Drug dealer)

- ➤ GOD REST YE MERRY, GENTLEMEN (Party 'til you die.)

- ➤ HAVE YOURSELF A MERRY LITTLE CHRISTMAS (I'm tapped out.)

- ➤ HERE WE COME A-WASSAILING (You ever see a body trampled by a herd of wassails? Not pretty.)

- ➤ LET IT SNOW! LET IT SNOW! LET IT SNOW! (Followed by the lesser-known LET ME SHOVEL! LET ME SHOVEL! LET ME DIE OF A HEART ATTACK!)

- ➤ ROCKIN' AROUND THE CHRISTMAS TREE (Don't come a-knockin' if the Christmas tree is rockin'!)

➢ RUDOLPH THE RED-NOSED REINDEER (Nothing worse than a boozing reindeer. They miss the roof, leave cookie crumbs, and crap where they want to.)

➢ SANTA BABY (Guess he went down more than the chimney.)

➢ SANTA CLAUS IS COMING TO TOWN & HERE COMES SANTA CLAUS (Santa got Viagra for Christmas, didn't he?)

➢ SILENT NIGHT (Yeah, like you can keep your mouth shut.)

➢ TWELVE DAYS OF CHRISTMAS (Cost me over a hundred grand to make this happen last year. Never again. The Leaping Lords stayed until mid-February.)

➢ WE THREE KINGS (Larry, Don, and Nosmo)

➢ WHAT CHILD IS THIS? (He doesn't look like me. I want a paternity test . . . now!)

➢ WHITE CHRISTMAS (Peruvian flake. Merry Christmas, yo.)

Snarkin' the Holidays

Christmas movies have pretty much always sucked. Completely filled with schmaltz and saccharin, and usually diabetic coma worthy, they also are clearly an exploitative moment when the filmmakers decided, "The hell with story, the hell with plot, I'm gettin' paid!" and make movies that are bland or boring or just plain bad.

"But Snark . . . I love [fill in the blank]!"

Yes, I know, there *are* a handful out there that never fail to tug at your heartstrings and that signal a beginning to the season . . . a season that really *needs* something to jump-start the mood. *It's a Wonderful Life*, the original *Miracle on 34th Street*, *A Charlie Brown Christmas*, the cartoon version of *How the Grinch Stole Christmas*—these are all terrific flicks. They can change your mood in an instant, even if you've seen them a hundred times.

But because they've hit a note in our collective psyche, every studio in Hollywood has tried to find a new replacement for these movies and 99 percent of the dreck that's resulted has failed miserably.

Here's a smattering of the Worst of the Worst:

➤ *Ernest Saves Christmas* – A yokel Christmas, based on a character that should have had the shelf life of a bunch of bananas. Santa's chauffeur? Really? This crapfest took about three minutes to conceptualize and slightly less to write.

➤ *Jack Frost* – Dead parent reincarnated as a live snowman. Yep. Could happen. Just no bonding nights around the fireplace, right? Oh wait, what's that you say? A Christmas miracle? Right. The only miracle here is that the filmmakers ever worked again.

➢ *Jingle All the Way* – The movie that comes closest to capturing the "real" spirit of Christmas: Get what you need at all costs. Fatherly love as shown through the procurement of an impossible-to-get action figure. Pit the dad against a stressed-out postal worker for the last one anywhere and watch the hilarity ensue. Starring Ahhnold, so you may need to use the subtitles.

➢ *All I Want for Christmas* – Starring Leslie Neilsen of *Naked Gun* fame, this one wanted to be the *Home Alone* of holiday movies, and failed miserably. (Some might put *Home Alone* on the list as a holiday movie . . . nope. While successful, the original and its sequels never quite accomplished mood changer status.) There is a good lesson to be learned, however: Kidnapping Santa is never a good way to bring your divorced parents back together.

➢ *Santa Claus Conquers the Martians* – Made in 1964, this movie tried to capitalize on the fear of alien life and extraterrestrials that had begun to build in the public. And if you're drunk enough or high enough, this movie can also be quite funny. It also begs audience participation, like the *The Rocky Horror Picture Show* . . . but I'm a little afraid of what you might want to throw instead of rice.

➢ *Eight Crazy Nights* – Adam Sandler's homage to Hanukkah. Even at a scant seventy-one minutes, this one is seventy-one minutes too long. There's enough scatalogical references and sophomoric humor to make it feel like it takes eight hours to watch.

> ➤ **Fred Claus** – Santa's dumber yet craftier older brother.
> When he gets in trouble, Nick bails him out. But he has to
> promise servitude at the North Pole . . . yikes. Where's
> Dr. Phil when you need him?

The last movie above actually leads into a subcategory group. It stars Vince Vaughn, who seems to have latched on to the whole holiday-means-box-office premise. So when you're on Netflix or at the video store, looking for that one movie that will help you find the spirit and the mood, here's another rule of thumb for your viewing protection:

No Vince Vaughn movies . . . no Ben Affleck movies . . . no Tim Allen movies . . . and beware Jim Carrey.

All have done multiple Christmas flicks and all are bad.

So rent the good ones again, make yourself a cup of nog and some popcorn, snuggle in, and watch for that moment when Clarence gets his wings or when Natalie gets her dream house . . . and be thankful you didn't opt for *The Santa Clause* . . . part 3, no less—now THAT'S a Christmas miracle.

Don't even get me started on television . . .

—THE AUTHOR

On the first night of Hanukkah, Jewish parents do something that can only be described as sadistic when they hand their child a top. A top. To play with. They call this top a dreidel. I know a fuckin' top when I see one. You can call it the king's nuts, I don't give a shit. Call it whatever you like, it's a top. A top is not something you play with. A top is not a toy. A toy is something you participate with. It'd be like the equivalent of if you had a young girl and she wanted a Barbie and you handed her a stick and said "Give it a name."

—LEWIS BLACK

✦✦

Christmas cards are just junk mail from people you know.

—PATRICIA MARX

✦✦✦

If you don't know about Hanukkah, I'll give you a brief little history. Hanukkah was conceived in 1957 by an optometrist in Nova Scotia, Dr. Maurice Tarnouer. And a lot of people think it's some sort of answer to Christmas to appease children who see their more powerful, affluent Christian friends able to celebrate this day. And they think it was somehow invented to appease those kids and say, "Well, you know, us Jews have our own thing. Here's eight days, so fuck you—how 'bout that?" And people who believe that are correct.

—DAVID CROSS

✦✦

Roses are things which Christmas is not a bed of.

—OGDEN NASH

✦✦✦

Christmas: Holiday in which the past or the future are not of as much interest as the present.

++

Christmas is a holiday that persecutes the lonely, the frayed, and the rejected.

—JIMMY CANNON

+++

When you compare Christmas to Hannukkah, Christmas is great. Hannukkah sucks! First night you get socks. Second night, an eraser, a notebook. It's a Back-to-School holiday!

—LEWIS BLACK

++

Four Reasons Hanukkah Sucks

1. **No good cards**: Rows and rows of Christmas cards and only one row of Hanukkah cards. Yeah, like you've got a hundred different people you want to send Hanukkah cards to . . . well, you'd better get them out in time because, after all, there only are EIGHT DAYS ON WHICH THEY CAN BE DELIVERED. The best Hanukkah card ever? "It's not your fault that Hanukkah sucks." End of story.

2. **The name**: Too many ways to spell and pronounce the name of the holiday. Yeah, I know. It's hard to say. Sounds funny too. Like you've got something stuck in your throat. And oy, boychick, is it hard to spell. Gee, is it *Hanukah* or *Chanuka* or *Chanukah* or *Chanukkah* or *Channukah* or *Hannukah* or *Hanukkah* or *Hanuka* or *Hanukka*

or *Hanaka* or *Haneka* or *Hanika* or *Khanukkah* . . . Please kill me now?

3. **Bad gifts**: Small. Large. Two medium. Small again. Large. Nothing. Small. Large(ish). Let's face it, Jewish parents don't really have much imagination. Not their fault. They've been struggling forever in the shadow of the Big One. For years. Their parents had the same problem. It's up to you to stop the madness.

4. **The music**: I once heard a story that Irving Berlin hated "White Christmas." Whattya wanna bet that that rumor got started by somebody who was pissed off that the only music associated with this holiday are a lame Adam Sandler ditty that's just dumb . . . and the dreidel song.

THE BOOK OF
CLICHÉS

Life and Death

Bite the dust / Bite your lip /
Bite the bullet / Bite your tongue—Come on, bite
something already, anything.

✦✦✦

Blood is thicker than water—and a lot harder to get out of clothing.

✦✦

Time heals all wounds—Bullshit. Drugs heal all wounds. Time does
nothing except go by.

✦✦✦

Blood money—Always welcome at many of your finer
establishments . . . otherwise Vegas would still be a desert.

✦✦

You've got blood on your hands—Don't say anything until you see a
lawyer.

✦✦✦

I spent my blood, sweat, and tears—and all I ever get is some schmuck
singing about a dumbass spinning wheel.

✦✦

Ashes to ashes, dust to dust—not to mention a few bone fragments, a
ligament or two . . . all things visceral, Sherlock.

✦✦✦

"The first man to compare the cheeks of a young woman to a rose was obviously a poet; the first to repeat it was possibly an idiot."
—SALVADORE DALI

Close only counts in horseshoes

✦

Cope with grief

✦

Years young

✦

Don't fly off the handle

✦

Everything's copasetic

✦

Final good-byes

✦

God help us

✦

Existential angst

✦

Moment of glory

✦

Twilight years

✦

Up the creek

✦

What comes around, goes around

✦

Life and limb

✦

Spring to life

✦

Take it easy

✦

Take the plunge

✦

These things happen

✦

Trials and tribulations

✦

Shallow grave

✦

You're gonna be dead meat—but given the choice, that's a whole lot better than being a dead vegetable, no? I mean, wouldn't you much rather be a hearty steak than a limp and flaccid broccoli?

++

The only thing certain are death and taxes—and Congress keeps trying to find ways to tax you long after you've died.

+++

He's gone, but not forgotten—Well . . . not yet. Give it a few days. It's like swallowing a cherry stone . . . it'll pass.

++

You can't take it with you —So I'm definitely going to spend every last dime I have before I go.

+++

What a way to go—As if there's a choice? I'll just wait for the next "death" to come around if you don't mind.

++

You only live once—Not necessarily, Mr. Bond.

+++

He was talking into his hat—Right . . . and we have to live with it after he puts it back on his head and walks away scot-free.

++

You throw filth on the living and flowers on the dead—Always good to see a man with priorities.

+++

He's bad to the bone—but always ready to party.

++

See no evil, hear no evil, speak no evil—Curious, nobody said a thing about "Do No Evil." Must be okay. Go to town.

+++

I'm in seventh heaven—Shootin' a little high there, Sparky . . . settle for the first or the second heaven. Lower expectations will curb some of the disappointment.

++

It's as hot as hell—What did you expect, the air-conditioned wing? Move over, Rasputin, and get a sweater.

+++

Like a bat out of hell—Must be some kinda baseball team, not just over the fence, but clear out of hell. Impressive.

++

Between the devil and the deep blue sea—what are you talking about here, a friggin' surfboard? Hang ten? That can't be right . . . Hangin' cloven hooves? Bingo. Gnarly, Luci baby.

+++

I catch hell if I do, and catch hell if I don't—so the hell with it, here comes your catcher.

++

I'm going to hell in a hand basket—Personally, I was hoping for a limo. Not a lot of room in a hand basket and I'm definitely bringin' a few folks with me.

+++

The Devil must be beating his wife—Not likely. We *all* know who wears the horns in that household.

++

Actions speak louder than words—To paraphrase Woody Allen, I never met anyone who didn't understand a slap in the face or a slug from a .45.

+++

All's fair in love and war—but most times you can't tell the two apart.

++

You only hurt the one you love—and that's because nobody else gives a shit what you do or would even put up with what you do.

+++

It's better to have loved and lost than never to have loved at all—Nah, not buyin' it, not one lil' bit.

++

Absence makes the heart grow fonder—Is it really the heart? Pretty sure absence makes the . . . hell, I don't know, can't remember now . . . maybe it was "abstinence" . . . what does abstinence make grow again?

+++

Is the Pope Catholic?—Yeah, yeah . . . and the bear shits in the woods and a chicken has lips . . . although, some Vatican watchers may actually question that first one.

++

You're off your rocker—Whew! Vince Neil must be breathing easier.

+++

You must be out of your mind—Clearly . . . and leaving my body on auto pilot. See you on the ground.

++

He's as neat as a pin—Some might whisper OCD. Just sayin'.

+++

Better the devil you know than the devil you don't—Actually, I'll stick with the devil I don't know and never have to meet.

++

He bought the farm—and this is an expression for dying? Old MacDonald had a farm and then a massive coronary and "bought the farm." Nice.

✦✦✦

Fools rush in where angels fear to tread—Always make it a practice to follow the fearless angels. They'll catch most of the flack.

✦✦

There's a sucker born every minute—and it looks like today is pretty much everybody's birthday.

✦✦✦

Ask me no questions and I'll tell you no lies—Huh? So what, you want me to ask you questions, then? 'Cos, the way you phrased that, it's fairly convoluted.

✦✦

Wisdom is not truth—Yeah, but then again, truth is pretty much open for debate.

✦✦✦

You're driving me insane—It's kind of a short drive. The gas meter didn't move at all.

✦✦

Always look out for number one—Although number two can really be a killer worth watching out for, too. Had to have that second bean burrito, right?

✦✦✦

I've got my back against the wall—Luckily, I have a blindfold in my pocket.

✦✦

Mind your manners—Or is it man your minors . . . make fun of
mourners . . . something like that.

+++

He's all eyes and ears—He may be all eyes but I'm having a whole lot
of trouble getting past those ears, Dumbo.

++

All is vanity—Who you kidding? You're vain. *All* is a laundry
detergent. Therefore, you're a laundry detergent. Makes sense, no?

+++

He went through the roof—Sort of solved our
problem . . . Elvis left the building, too.

++

You have to turn the other cheek—What . . . and get that one slapped
too? Okay, c'mon, I'm a man, I can take it. Hey! Not so hard.

+++

You need to read the handwriting on the wall—With your luck,
they'll end up being gang tags and you'll end up getting your ass
kicked.

++

What a way to go—Actually, does it even matter? It all pretty much
ends up the same, anyway . . . and you're dead a long time.

+++

Name your poison—Does anyone ever get that? Yeah, let's see . . . I
think I'll go with cyanide, because arsenic always gives me a nasty
heartburn.

++

Make it down and dirty—Despite paying $10,000 for a coffin, it's the way we're all going to end up. Down and dirty. No other way *to* make it.

+++

She could be her evil twin—and really, how will you ever tell them apart?

++

The Devil must be beating his wife—Hey, her parents warned her he was no good. Some kids never listen. You'd have thought the horns, tail, and all that fire would have given it away.

+++

Don't look back, the Devil might be gaining—Doesn't really matter if you look back or not, he's pretty much got this race all sewn up.

++

It's as easy as 1-2-3—Don't overestimate yourself, Einstein . . . these days, that's just beta testing.

+++

He's on an emotional roller coaster—More like emotional bumper cars, careening from one crash to the next. Should have worn a helmet.

++

To be honest/To tell you the truth—So what . . . everything beforehand has been a lie? Or is it that you usually lie your ass off.

+++

Cliché Hall of Famer #1 – Ben Franklin*

"Beer is living proof that God loves us and wants us to be happy."

"Little boats should keep near shore."

"He that goes a borrowing goes a sorrowing."

"Those things that hurt, instruct."

"Men forget but never forgive. Women forgive but never forget."

"Originality is the art of concealing your sources."

"Life's tragedy is that we get old too soon and wise too late."

The Great Outdoors

"Our writers are full of clichés just as old barns are full of bats. There is obviously no rule about this, except that anything that you suspect of being a cliché undoubtedly is one and had better be removed."
—WOLCOTT GIBBS

When life gives you lemons, make lemonade—or open a stand. Do *something*. Life is clearly thirsty. Not real big on taking the subtle hints, are ya Sparky?

♦♦

When life gives you lemons—shut the fuck up. It could easily give you broccoli. You want broccoli? Yeah, that's what I thought . . .

♦♦♦

An apple never falls far from the tree— and isn't it amazing how many bad apples one tree can produce?

♦♦

Apple of my eye—but a pain in my ass.

♦♦♦

You're beating a dead horse—but it still pisses off PETA.

♦♦

A bird in the hand is worth two in the bush—But a bush in the hand is typically anywhere from $50 to $100.

♦♦♦

She's as blind as a bat—But hey, that's what you get from sleeping upside down.

++

A green thumb

+

You can't learn to swim without getting in the water

+

You must row with the oars that you have

+

A nice day for a picnic

+

Taking the scenic route

+

A cloudless sky

+

Dog days

+

Early-morning hours

+

Yer all wet

+

Barking up the wrong tree

+

Tell your story walking

+

Weather the storm

+

Many moons

+

Fun in the sun

+

It's a one-horse town—and they just handed me the shovel.

+++

That'll happen when pigs fly—Hey, I've been stuck on many an airline trip where I could have sworn . . .

++

You can't teach an old dog new tricks—Nah, he'll just piss on the rug and hump your leg like always.

+++

When you lie down with lions, you wake up with fleas—Sorry, not going to happen, any lying down will be the last thing you do . . . but look on the bright side, the lions won't have to eat for another few days.

++

Naked as a jaybird—Right, because all the other birds are so dressed to the nines   what the hell does that cliché mean, anyway?

+++

Once bitten, twice shy—Except if you're one of those Animal Planet hosts   then once bitten means higher ratings and a second season renewal.

++

Waiting with baited breath—Because I'm what? A fish? Try some Listerine or Scope maybe . . . extra-strength with bait-removing particles . . .

+++

The world is not my oyster—Nor is it any other kind of bivalve.

++

You're barking up the wrong tree—Right, because dog behavior is so scientifically calculated . . . want to buy a picture of Einstein licking himself?

+++

If you build a better mousetrap, the world will beat a path to your door—Dropping off every friggin' mouse they can find.

++

It shines like a diamond in a goat's ass—Tell me, just how do you know exactly how shiny that is? (And where did this cliché come from?)

+++

Lie down with dogs and wake up with fleas—The alternative being lying down with pussies and getting crabs?

++

His bark is worse than his bite—Really? Given how much of a jerk-off he is, that must be some frickin' bark.

+++

It's like the blind leading the blind—A reminder to never buy a "slightly used" seeing eye dog that's advertised as "having great hearing."

++

Birds of a feather flock together—Birds of different feathers end up on ladies' hats or as integral parts of sex toys.

+++

He's the cat's pajamas—Yes, with an open flap in the back so he can lick himself.

++

We were crammed in like sardines—Thankfully, we were able to coat ourselves in a really high-grade olive oil.

+++

Even a blind squirrel finds an acorn sometimes—More often than not, he finds the bottom of a set of Michelin radials first.

++

When the lion is dead, the hare jumps on his back—Making all those "play dead" lessons pay off pretty good for the lions, no?

+++

You can't make a silk purse out of a sow's ear—Hey, give it time. I hear Bloomies is selling Sow's Ear purses for serious bucks.

++

A rose by any other name would smell as sweet—I guess you can call them what you want . . . but I guarantee that sending your wife a dozen American Beauty long-stemmed "spider warts" will not get you laid.

+++

Make like a tree and leave—I've been in like, a million forests, and I've never once seen a tree up and walk away . . . so what exactly are you talking about?

♦♦

As clear as mud. As cold as ice. As common as dirt. As delicate as a flower. As pure as snow—Okay, I get it, Captain Obvious. How about as pointless as this stupid cliché?

♦♦♦

She's as cold as ice—and twice as slippery. And your tongue always gets stuck to her.

♦♦

She's as delicate as a flower—Nothing delicate about that smell, though.

♦♦♦

As fresh as a daisy—Hey there, Sparky, not for nuthin', but maybe you should get your nose checked out by an ENT . . . real soon.

♦♦

Curiosity killed the cat—Well, really, what did that cat expect, after waking Curiosity up at that hour of the morning and jumping on the bed while trying to get under the covers?

♦♦♦

If a dog is man's best friend—Is a cat man's snotty, passive-aggressive ex-girlfriend?

♦♦

I'm so hungry, I could eat a horse—Yeah, well, I ate a big breakfast so a pony will be more than enough for me, thank you.

+++

It's not the heat, it's the humidity—Made all the more unbearably banal by that ridiculous reference to the humidity. And it's still frickin' hot, Swami.

++

I'm as nervous as a long-tailed cat in a living room full of rockers—I'd be nervous too if I were a YouTube video waiting to happen.

+++

Any port in any storm—Whatever it takes to shiver me timbers, Matey.

++

As honest as the day is long—We talkin' regular days or Winter Soltice days?

+++

As pure as the driven snow—That big-ass Saint Bernard with the weak bladder has been by here, huh? And what's up with the "driven" stuff? Too lazy to walk?

++

You can't change a leopard's spots—Kind of a roundabout way to say that some things are permanent, don't cha think? Maybe you can simplify things a tad . . . that'd be a nice change. Start small maybe?

+++

There's more than one way to skin a cat—Really, because why? There's that much cat-skinning going on these days that you need more than one way? What is this, one of those new-fangled arts and crafts classes?

++

He's a big fish in a small pond—Well, he ain't such a big fish but the smell is certainly on the "big fish" level.

+++

She treated me like a dog—Cool . . . fed me, walked me . . . rubbed my belly. Picked up the dump I took on the sidewalk. Kinda cool being her dog. Not liking the leash, though.

++

He went whole hog—Next time he gets that way, truss him up, throw him on a spit, and roast him slowly for a bunch of hours . . . should take him down a peg.

+++

Never pet a burning dog—A truism originally uttered by Phil, the one-armed, badly charred dog trainer.

++

Haven't seen that in a coon's age—Hey . . . stop right there . . . not racist . . . it's a raccoon. Really. Look it up.

+++

Running dog lackey—Just what the world needs now, a redundant Chinese derivative expression of hate . . . because, like most Chinese expressions, we don't have a clue as to what it means. But definitely add "in bed" to the end of it.

++

Don't be a scaredy-cat—Leave it to you to try to find some benefit to getting the crap scared out of you. No thanks, I'll just wait here.

+++

See you later, alligator—That rhyme maybe worked a little when you were four years old, Tupac . . . now it just tells me you're not ready for any kind of poetry slam any time soon.

++

He's the south end of a north-bound horse.—Dress it up all you want, but getting to the point, he's still an enormous horse's ass.

+++

I quit smoking, cold turkey—Does that make me hungry as a bear, cranky as a mule, and horny as a tomcat? Right, I'm a frickin' zoo. But I really don't miss it in the least . . . uh, mind if I lick your ashtray?

++

If you can build a better mousetrap—Let's see . . . spring-loaded kill bar, piece of cheese, and . . . well, that's it. What do you want to add, Rube Goldberg, a remote control?

+++

What's good for the goose is good for the gander—So, even geese have to deal with breaking the glass ceiling . . . Hard to watch, though. Slender necks and all . . .

✦✦

Gonna party until the cows come home—Have you ever seen a cow after a debauched night out? Not a pretty sight. Big, red bloodshot hide . . . udder disaster.

✦✦✦

I want to kill two birds with one stone—Try tying the two of them together with weighted rocks . . . works like a charm every time.

✦✦

I'm in hog heaven—Maybe, but pretty sure you're gonna wake up in "Ugly as a Pig" hell.

✦✦✦

Hey, is it hot enough for you?—Usually asked when it's too friggin' hot for anything that doesn't live in the water. No, I'm Beezlebub . . . could use it turned up a few notches.

✦✦

It's not the heat, it's the humidity—What are you, Al Roker? It's a nasty combination of both . . . made worse by comments like that.

✦✦✦

Yeah, but it's a dry heat—Here's an idea . . . turn your oven up to 110 and stick your head in there for a few hours. If you're still alive after, I'll agree.

✦✦

Great Moments in Clichés – The Arts

"Eighty percent of success is showing up."

–Woody Allen

"Anything worth doing is worth overdoing."

–Mick Jagger

"Dream as if you'll live forever, live as if you'll die today."

–James Dean

"Success is falling nine times and getting up ten."

–Jon Bon Jovi

"We're born alone, we live alone, we die alone. Only through our love and friendship can we create the illusion for the moment that we're not alone."

–Orson Welles

"You know you are getting old when the candles cost more than the cake."

–Bob Hope

"Truth is like the sun. You can shut it out for a time, but it ain't goin' away."

–Elvis Presley

Time will tell—Time will tell nothing . . . if time knows what's good for it . . . or time will be sleeping with the fishes.

+++

They say music has the power to soothe the savage beast—Yeah, but it won't keep them from tearing you limb from limb . . . soothingly, though.

++